THE

7-day

CHRISTIAN

How Living Your Beliefs Every Day
Can Change the World

BRAD WILCOX

ENSIGN
PEAK

To my dear friend Ron Riley—
truly a 7-day Christian

© 2014 Bradley Ray Wilcox and Deborah G. Gunnel Wilcox Family Trust

Visit us at EnsignPeakPublishing.com

Library of Congress Cataloging-in-Publication Data
(CIP data on file)
ISBN 978-1-60907-851-5

Printed in the United States of America
R. R. Donnelley, Crawfordsville, IN

10   9   8   7   6   5   4   3   2   1

CONTENTS

ACKNOWLEDGMENTS

This book simply would not have been finished without the help of two friends, Sharon Black and Eula Monroe. Their feedback and input on each chapter made the book much stronger than it would have been. I appreciate their unique perspectives and finely honed skills as writers. Most important, I admire the daily choices they make to live their beliefs with integrity. They are examples to me and all who know them.

Wendee Wilcox Rosborough and David Wilcox, two of my children, were willing to respond to my rough drafts. I am thankful to have their fingerprints throughout the book. As always, I also appreciate my wife, Debi, for her selfless support and love.

Thanks to Chris Schoebinger, who first approached me with the idea for this book and challenged me to stretch beyond my comfort zone. I admire Emily Watts, who has been my talented editor and faithful friend for many years. Additional thanks to Brett C. Sanders, who always believes in me and gives valuable feedback; Sheryl Dickert Smith, who created the cover; and Richard Erickson, the project's art director. My life has also been forever enriched by the "Aussie 11" and the Randall family—a wonderful team of friends who have been blessed with the opportunities to create some amazing memories together. I love you all.

INTRODUCTION

I grew up in Ethiopia, Africa. When I shared this with the sixth graders I used to teach, they didn't believe me. One girl said, "No way! You did *not* grow up in Ethiopia!" I assured her I did. She responded, "No way! You're not skinny enough!" All this young lady had ever heard about Ethiopia was that people there were starving, and I certainly didn't look like I qualified!

Throughout the year I shared many memories of Africa with my students. I wanted them to realize that there is more to Ethiopia than the starving children their moms told them about when they didn't want to finish their vegetables. I shared with them Ethiopia's long and proud history, the people's love of music and family, and the happiness that many experience even without the material possessions we enjoy. In Ethiopia I saw the heartbreaking effects of poverty and the incredible value of literacy and education. However, there was one life-changing lesson that I couldn't share in public school: In Ethiopia, I learned what it means to be a Christian.

Many are surprised to discover that Ethiopia is a predominantly Christian country. The Coptic Christian tradition began in the first century in Egypt and spread to Ethiopia. I remember many devoted people who had the Coptic cross tattooed on their foreheads. When I asked my parents about this, they explained that these people marked themselves with the cross to let everyone know they were Christians. I said, "Then I want one because I am a Christian too." My parents then taught me that it is not a cross marked on your forehead or worn on a chain around your neck that makes you a Christian. It is what is inside—the way you feel, the way you believe, and the way you live—that indicates your relationship with God. As Mike McKinley wrote, "Simply saying that you are a Christian doesn't mean you really are one" (*Am I Really a Christian?* 16).

Many textbooks attribute the early rise of Christianity to Constantine. Earlier Roman leaders had persecuted Christians—especially Roman converts, who were seen as traitors for going against their own culture. The Roman Empire was divided, unstable, and at war with itself. Constantine wanted to unite the Empire once again. It is said he had a vision in which he was told that he would conquer Rome under the sign of the cross. The leader ordered the symbol of Christ to be placed on the shields of all his soldiers and vowed that if they were victorious, he would become a Christian. They were, and, true to his word, he was baptized.

In reality, Christianity does not owe its survival to Constantine, but to ordinary people like you and me. Christianity spread and flourished not because of a dramatic battle and painted shields, but because of the faithfulness of early converts. These were men and women who believed and lived by their beliefs—no matter the cost.

Historians debate whether Constantine's conversion was sincere or just politically expedient. Did Christianity become acceptable because he joined, or did he join because it had grown so acceptable? Did Constantine have a vision or simply enough vision to see that he could use this growing movement to his advantage? We may never know. The fact that is beyond debate is this: Everyday Christians living their religion every day changed the world.

The Christian doctrines of charity and hope must have been appealing to people who had spent their lives dealing with the upheavals of war and revolution. Christian promises of the possibility of a bright future for all people, regardless of class or position, must have sounded wonderful to the poor who struggled to feed and shelter their families. But who would have taken time to listen to Christian doctrine without having first noticed the fruits of Christian discipleship—the high morals, pure motives, self-discipline, and unity within the Christian community? People saw Christians rescue babies from the infanticide so common in the pagan populations. When deadly epidemics wiped out entire communities and the healthy ran in fear, Christians remained to care for the needy—including those who were not of their faith.

Who would have taken time to listen to Christian doctrine without having first noticed the fruits of Christian discipleship—the high morals, pure motives, self-discipline, and unity within the Christian community?

Chris and Ted Stewart wrote, "Despite the efforts of the pagan emperors to destroy them, [the early Christians'] willingness to serve the empire, as well as their reputation for virtue, law-abiding behavior, and strength of character had brought them considerable goodwill" (*The Miracle of Freedom,* 130).

Now let's fast-forward many centuries. As in its early years, Christianity today faces great challenges and opposition. Some Christians are being imprisoned and threatened physically. Some are marginalized and misjudged socially because of their beliefs and the negative perceptions people have of them. In their book *UnChristian,* David Kinnaman and Gabe Lyons have documented pop culture's alarming perceptions of Christians and the "intense hostility" such perceptions have generated (38). They wrote, "Many young believers say that in some circumstances they are reluctant to admit they are Christians. . . . They feel that raising the

Christian flag would actually undermine their ability to connect with people and to maintain credibility with them" (35). Similarly, George Yancey wrote, "I have substantiated the reality that religious and political conservatives face a level of rejection that other social groups do not experience" (*Compromising Scholarship*, 181). I know of university leaders who have banned Christian groups from their campuses. I know of a Christian pharmacist who was required to fill prescriptions that went against her own personal religious convictions. I know of a wedding photographer who was fined heavily and whose business was later boycotted because he chose not to photograph a ceremony that contradicted his beliefs. Many of us may not have faced such overt threats to our religious freedom, but at the very least, we know how it feels to end up on the wrong side of a "politically correct" conversation.

We are approaching another turning point in history. Once again, the world is divided, unstable, and at war with itself. It's time for another rise in Christianity. Kinnaman and Lyons wrote, "This won't happen if we try simply to make ourselves look good. The reputation of the Christian faith should never be managed or spin-doctored. . . . Your life shows other people what God is like" (*UnChristian*, 38).

We don't need another

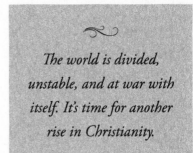

The world is divided, unstable, and at war with itself. It's time for another rise in Christianity.

Constantine or another victory at the Milvian Bridge on the Tiber River. We need an "awakening of authenticity . . . so that . . . the world will see real love and sacrifice and courage in the service of Christ" (John Piper, *Finally Alive,* 18). We need more genuine Christians who have the courage to be Christlike. We need more faithful disciples who are willing to let Christ transform their thoughts, feelings, actions, and motives. We need more believing and behaving disciples—faithful men and women who are ready to stand up and stand together to change the world as early Christians did—one renewed friendship, one warm embrace, one sincere compliment, one compassionate act, one righteous choice at a time.

CHAPTER ONE

"IF ANY MAN WILL DO HIS WILL, HE SHALL KNOW"

Is there a God?" This may be one of the world's most frequently asked questions. I've heard it from people who are religious and nonreligious, educated and uneducated, rich and poor, young and old, in private and in public. It is articulated with great intensity by sincere seekers of truth, but it has been demeaned to the level of a joke by cynical comedians. One way or another, everyone seems to take a turn asking this question of all questions.

Some answer with an emphatic *yes,* others with an equally emphatic *no.* Many waver between opinions, depending on the occasion, while some claim the answer doesn't even matter. But it does. Our response affects what we believe about life here and now as well as in the hereafter. It affects how we value and interact with other people and also how we see our own potential, our ability to make positive changes, and our motives for even trying.

THE GREAT DEBATE

Faithful Christians provide evidence for God's existence—the scriptures, the wonders of creation, the upward yearnings they feel, miraculous conversions, and answers they have received to their prayers. The faithless counter with their own evidence. They claim scriptures are myths and fables, creation results from big bangs and natural selection, upward impulses are self-delusion or prelingual memories. Answers to prayer are nothing more than self-fulfilling prophecy, coincidence, or fate.

The faithful ask, "What about conscience, our inborn moral compass?" The faithless declare that conscience is merely the product of social conditioning. The faithful ask, "What about our tendency to experience guilt and our ability to differentiate between regret for mistakes and remorse for sin?" The faithless respond that these are merely the result of indoctrination.

Back and forth rages the debate, with each round becoming more and more intense. Advocates on both sides demand tolerance for their own viewpoints but sometimes offer little tolerance for the viewpoints of others. What ultimately determines an individual's choice? Surely it varies, as each must make his or her own decision. But one piece of evidence that has been crucial for me as I step back and consider the options is that I *can* step back and consider the options. To me the very possibility for debate is strong evidence that a Supreme Being does exist—one who has created us in His image and allows us to reason and make choices. I don't see plants and animals having discussions about whether or not God exists. Simply being complex enough to consider both possibilities sets humans apart.

Can evolution alone truly account for our complexity and unpredictability? Human abilities and potential cannot be reduced to anything that natural selection alone would have called for. Consider how profoundly we can love, how openly we can cry, how boisterously we can laugh, how deeply we can hurt, and how boundlessly we can feel joy. In addition to feeling these strong emotions for ourselves, we experience empathy that allows us to feel these same emotions on behalf of others. We can feel grief at another's suffering; we can feel joy at another's success. This common humanity goes far beyond self-awareness and survival of the fittest.

> *To me the very possibility for debate is strong evidence that a Supreme Being does exist— one who has created us in His image and allows us to reason and make choices.*

Animals eat for survival, but people can seek out and appreciate a fine restaurant. Animals use smell to hunt, but people can use the same sense to savor moments and later trigger memories. As humans, not only can we separate our actions from ourselves, we can reflect on them. What animal can say, "Such behavior wasn't like me"? What animal is capable of honest introspection? We are different because we can conceive of a better version of ourselves. What animal can redefine itself in this way?

We can step outside ourselves and consider questions that go far beyond the bounds of our own life experiences. At times we ponder such questions with fleeting curiosity. At other times we literally ache to learn and to know. How many chemical reactions can create such meaning as they take place? This ability seems evidence enough for me to choose to believe there is a God.

THE CHOICE

Others may come to the same conclusion and believe in God's existence, but our search for understanding does not stop with this decision. What evidence do we have that God does anything more than exist? A Supreme Being could exist and be completely apathetic, distant, and cold. We could just be a few more of His creations about which He has no concern. Perhaps God may even be selfish and cruel. What evidence do we have that God is not a tyrant who delights in torturing us? Certainly many who have experienced trials and heartaches have questioned God's love. Once again, one of the decision factors for me as I consider God's attributes is that I have multiple options and the opportunity to choose. My freedom to choose seems an assurance that God is benevolent, caring, and concerned rather than controlling.

My friend Wendy Ulrich wrote, "Faith is a choice we make amid alternatives, not what is left over after all competing worldviews have been neatly eliminated" ("The Presence of an Absence," 178). Consider how evenly the evidence of God's existence or nonexistence is displayed. To me, that distribution says something about God's character. It appears He doesn't want to manipulate the evidence unfairly in either direction—not because He is apathetic about what I believe but because He wants me to be completely free to make my own choice.

Freedom brings with it great risks and the possibility of pain, but it is absolutely necessary for progress and fulfillment. Because God wants us to have peace and joy, He desires us to believe in Him, but if the evidence were too clear in His favor, we would be "forced" to accept it as we are "forced" to accept the law of gravity. To me, one of the clearest evidences of God's goodness is that He does not prove himself to us beyond all possibility of doubt. The fact that He allows compelling evidence on both sides of the argument of His existence preserves and honors my freedom. Growth and happiness are totally dependent on my choices, and since God allows me freedom to choose, I can conclude that He desires my growth and happiness! He may ultimately want me to believe, but more important, it appears He wants me *to want* to believe.

Terryl and Fiona Givens have written, "There must be grounds for doubt as well as belief, in order to render the choice more truly a choice. . . . When faith is a freely chosen gesture, it expresses something essential about the self" (*The God Who Weeps*, 4–5).

In the end, believers find it more reasonable to believe in God than to believe in a never-ending stream of "coincidences" necessary to account for life on earth. They do not believe that by chance the earth came into existence a perfect distance from the sun or that by random luck it functions with a rare elliptical orbit and tilt that allow life to exist. They do not think it is a twist of fate that we have a moon at the precise distance to allow for tides that sustain life instead of destroying it. To believers, the ratio of protons and electrons in each atom and the complexity of each body system and organ are much more than good fortune.

Nevertheless, nonbelievers claim that in the vastness of the universe the probability of such twists of fate all coming together at the exact same time may not be as outrageous as it seems. To them, a chain of random accidents is more reasonable than a belief in God.

While everyone argues for his or her side, the fact that there are two sides and freedom to choose between them makes a difference to me. There is strong and compelling evidence on both sides of the argument of God's existence, but neither side can "prove" anything beyond the possibility of doubt. To me, this balance of pros and cons says much about God's goodness. I choose to believe that God exists and that He cares because He obviously values my freedom enough to let me make that choice and live with the consequences. He wins my devotion, praise, and worship precisely because He refuses to force me to make these offerings.

We can believe God exists partly because He gives us

the precious capacity to contemplate His existence. We can believe God cares about our choices because He gives us complete freedom to make them. But is that enough? Surely a God who exists and cares must desire something more from us and for us. Surely a God who endowed us with capacity and preserved our freedom wants us to use that freedom to develop our capacity. Surely He doesn't want us to make just *any* choices, but to make wise and deliberate choices to draw closer to Him.

FAITH, OBEDIENCE, AND KNOWLEDGE

I attended a meeting at which the man directing finished his remarks with the words, "May you be at peace with God whatever you conceive Him to be." I'm sure his words were chosen carefully in an effort to not offend anyone, but they left me unsettled. Are we really at liberty to conceive God? Can we invent Him, alter Him, or change Him to fit our ideas? Isn't it more important to seek to know Him as He is and allow Him to influence us?

Jesus taught, "And this is life eternal, that they might know thee the only true God, and Jesus Christ, whom thou hast sent" (John 17:3). We can come to know God by following Jesus (see Matthew 16:24; Luke 9:23). Jesus explained, "If any man will do his will, he shall know of the doctrine, whether it be of God, or whether I speak of myself" (John 7:17).

Such knowledge is possible for those ready to live on a higher plane. God doesn't want this life to be an endless debate or a guessing game. We can know for ourselves, and one way in which we prepare ourselves to receive this knowledge is to *do* God's will. No wonder David Kinnaman and Gabe Lyons have written, "The truest knowing comes in the doing" (*UnChristian*, 225). True faith inevitably leads to action. Faith in Jesus Christ always leads to repentance and change. Repentance and obedience are not replacements for faith but extensions of it—substance of our acceptance of Christ and evidence that Christ is working with, in, and through us. John F. MacArthur, Jr., wrote, "Obedience . . . is the inevitable characteristic of those who are saved" (*Faith Works,* 121).

The faithless see commandments as inconveniences or pointless burdens. The faithful see them as divine gifts from a loving God who is helping us know Him. The faithless see commandments as limiting their freedom. The faithful see them as insuring and expanding it.

> *The faithless see commandments as inconveniences or pointless burdens. The faithful see them as divine gifts from a loving God who is helping us know Him.*

When my children were young, I was asked to direct a study-abroad program in New Zealand as part of my work. Our family had a wonderful experience living in Auckland

14

and traveling throughout that amazing country. One day my son Russell, who was sixteen years old at the time, came to me and said, "Dad, bungee jumping was invented here."

"Cool!" I responded.

"Dad, you don't get it. Bungee jumping was *invented* here."

"Cool!" I said again.

Then Russell dropped the bomb: "So I have to go bungee jumping."

"No," I said. "You do *not* have to go bungee jumping!"

"But, Dad, it was invented here."

I said, "I know where the electric chair was invented, but that doesn't mean—"

"Please, Dad," Russell interrupted. "I really want to go bungee jumping."

Over the next few weeks he persisted in his pestering and pleading until I finally gave in. I had seen bungee towers in the United States at amusement parks and in grocery store parking lots—always surrounded by plenty of air mattresses at the bottom. I thought, "How dangerous can it really be?" Then I discovered that's not the way they do it in New Zealand—land of no lawsuits! They jump out of helicopters. They jump off bridges into rivers. They jump off sheer mountain cliffs with no air mattresses at the bottom. There are only rocks (and tombstones).

I still remember the day that Russell, his older sister, and some friends decided to throw themselves off a mountainside in Queenstown. They took their turns being strapped into the harness that was attached to the bungee cord. To me it looked like an old-fashioned corset that was cinched up tight in the back. When the man working the jump put Russell into the harness, he tightened it to the point that my son squeaked out, "Dad, I can't breathe. It's too tight."

My immediate response was, "It is *not* too tight!" I actually didn't know how tight it was, but I wanted it tighter! Why? Because I wanted him to live through the experience. I didn't want my son to snap his back.

How foolish would a person be to remove the harness before jumping, saying, "This harness is too tight. I want to be free!" He's free all right, but for how long? His freedom ends—and it ends very abruptly, painfully, and permanently. Because Russell was willing to put up with the tight harness, he was the one who was truly free—free to jump, which he did (Superman style)! He was free to buy the very expensive video of the experience, which he did. He was free to show it to everyone who dared visit our home for the next year, which he did. Russell was free *because* of the harness, not *in spite* of it. God's rules, expectations, standards, and commandments are not restricting cords that bind us down. They are the bungee cords that allow us to fly!

WORSHIPFUL EMULATION

God patiently allows us to debate His existence, but He certainly doesn't want that to be the end of our learning experience. He grants us time to ponder about His character, but only for a greater purpose. Consider the situation in reverse. God doesn't spend all His time wondering whether we exist. He knows it. He spends less time questioning our characters and more time shaping them. Just as He knows us perfectly, He desires that we come to know Him. "Ask and it shall be given you; seek, and ye shall find; knock, and it shall be opened unto you" (Matthew 7:7).

Asking, seeking, knocking—in each application God is asking us to *do* something. Too many say, "You can't know God exists. Even if He does, you can't know His character or intentions. You can believe, but you can't know." However, Jesus taught, "And ye shall know the truth, and the truth shall make you free" (John 8:32). My own experience has confirmed to me that as I strive to do God's will, I have come to know Him better. And the better I know Him, the more I love Him and desire to serve Him and emulate Him.

Many in the world look at God's commandments as true-false or multiple-choice options on a test He is giving us. I don't see them as God's test as much as His lesson. I don't see God grading us as much as He is educating us. Perhaps the key to living the way we believe is realizing that ultimately we are not limited to believing. By living lives consistent with our faith, we can know. And when we know, we can live securely and joyfully in worshipful emulation of our Lord—not just on Sunday, but 7 days a week.

CHAPTER TWO

ANYONE CAN
WRITE A STORY

Chloe Vroman was a remarkable teacher who was years ahead of her time. Back when most high school English teachers were diagramming sentences and drilling parts of speech, Mrs. Vroman was teaching us to write by having us write. On the first day of class she announced, "We're not going to play the typical school game in which I assign a topic, you write a paper, and then I bleed all over it with my red pen and pass it back with a grade. That's not how real writers write." And rumor whispered that she was a real writer. Mrs. Vroman helped us select our own topics. She met with us one-on-one to discuss our writing and provide feedback. Most important, she had us share our writing with others. "I am not your audience," she would say over and over. "Your audience is out there. I am just helping you get ready to submit your writing for publication." And submit we did. We submitted to magazines, newspapers, and every writing contest Mrs. Vroman ever heard about.

MY STORY

I remember one day when Mrs. Vroman came into class and said, "*Guideposts* magazine is sponsoring a youth writing contest, and I think some of you should consider entering." I had seen the little inspirational magazine in the waiting room at my doctor's office and had read some articles in it, but I hesitated at the thought of a national contest. I didn't mind entering the PTA writing contest because everyone who submitted received a doughnut. I didn't mind sending in my patriotic essay for the local freedom festival contest because everyone who did got some free tickets to the carnival. But enter a national contest? I decided to pass.

Everyone in our class must have felt the same way I did; no one entered. When Mrs. Vroman found out, she was so upset she decreed that entering the contest was no longer optional. "Now it is a requirement!" she announced. "Those who don't submit a story will not get a grade out of my class and will not graduate from high school!" I didn't even know if a teacher could do something like that, but I wasn't going to wait around to find out. That weekend I wrote my story, which my mom helped me edit, and sent it off to *Guideposts*.

A few months later I received a letter informing me that I had placed in the top ten for the contest. I took the letter to school and showed it to Mrs. Vroman, who screamed, "You're in the top ten!"

I said, "There were probably only *eleven* entries, and they were probably all from *our* class because you forced everyone to enter!"

"No, Brad," she assured me, "this is a big deal." Mrs. Vroman rushed off to call the offices of *Guideposts* in New York City. When she returned, she reported there had been thousands of entries from all across the country, and I really was in the top ten! Wow! Mrs. Vroman said that the senior editor, Van Varner, was planning a trip around the country to personally visit all the finalists.

It was kind of exciting when Mr. Varner showed up in my hometown. He met my family and Mrs. Vroman. I got to eat lunch with him and the principal. I even got my picture in the newspaper. As I drove Mr. Varner around, he was full of questions. He asked about my community and school. He asked me about my family and our beliefs. He asked about how I wrote my story. When I got to the part about Mrs. Vroman forcing the whole class to enter, he was laughing hysterically. I didn't think the possibility of not graduating from high school was all that funny, but he sure seemed to enjoy it.

In return, I asked him a few questions of my own, like who would be judging the contest.

"Have you ever heard of Catherine Marshall or Corrie ten Boom?" he asked.

I hadn't. I cringe now when I think back on the moment.

How did I not recognize Catherine Marshall, the best-selling author of the book *Christy?* How had I not heard of Corrie ten Boom, who wrote *The Hiding Place* based on her own horrific experiences in a Nazi concentration camp during World War II? Today I certainly know who these amazing women are, and I feel honored to think that these authors read—and liked—my little story.

Before Mr. Varner left town to meet the other nine finalists, he asked, "Brad, do you know why I came to visit you?" I was stumped. I guess deep down I knew it was part of his job, but I still figured the main reason he had flown all the way from New York City was just because he wanted to meet me.

Mr. Varner continued, "*Guideposts* is no ordinary magazine. It is a Christian magazine based on Christian values. I needed to make sure that the story you submitted was not plagiarized. But more important, I needed to make sure that you as an author are really trying to live the values espoused by the magazine."

Mr. Varner went on, "You see, Brad, anyone can write a story about Christian values. It's a whole different thing to live the values you write about." I agreed. It was easy to see how awkward it would be to give me an award and then have me end up in some big scandal, but I hadn't known the whole visit was a test. I knew I had not plagiarized the story, but the second question was a more complicated one. Was I consistently living the way I claimed to believe?

Mrs. Vroman had forced this high school senior to write

a story. Now Mr. Varner had forced this high school senior into a moment of honest introspection. I would soon
be graduating and starting college. Was I going to continue
to live the way I had been taught, even when parents and
teachers were not there? Were Christian values things I lived
or just things I wrote stories about?

Not long after Mr. Varner's visit, I received a telegram—
that's right, a telegram. I tell teenagers today that a telegram
was an early—and very expensive—text message. Dr.
Norman Vincent Peale (now, *that* name I recognized),
founder of *Guideposts* and author of *The Power of Positive
Thinking,* wrote me my own personal, powerful, positive
telegram: I had won first place in the contest.

My story would be published in the May issue of the
magazine, and my picture would be on the cover. My story
would be picked up by news syndicates worldwide and
translated into other languages! I had won a total of $6,000
in scholarships. With my very expensive text message in
hand, I rushed off to find my parents and tell them the
good news. I also wanted to find Mrs. Vroman to thank her.
After all, this was her fault! Perhaps more important, I knew
I needed to thank Mr. Varner for reminding me that values
should not just be *talked about* but *lived.* Anyone can write a
story filled with characters, but it takes courage to live a life
filled with character. Anyone can write a story and portray
himself in an honorable light, but it takes true integrity to
live honorably in the light.

Dr. Stephen R. Covey was a man who lived such a

life. He wrote *The 7 Habits of Highly Effective People,* and he lived those habits. I had the rare opportunity to see Dr. Covey on both public and private occasions. I was impressed to find that whether he was speaking before groups of thousands or sitting in his home with his family, he was the same. Whether he was consulting with presidents and world leaders or talking one-on-one with young college students, he was the same.

I once asked Dr. Covey which of his books he considered his best. He said, "Any author's best book is his own life." In other words, anyone can write a story. Had Stephen R. Covey been consulting with Mr. Varner? No, but they had both learned a lesson we all must ultimately learn: It is one thing to profess noble beliefs and another to live them—even when living them is not easy or convenient. From high school to now, the process of aligning my behaviors and beliefs has always been easier when I have felt a sense of urgency, mission, and integrity.

A SENSE OF URGENCY

I was in attendance when Stephen R. Covey was speaking at a university to a group of ambitious business students. "How many want to be rich?" he asked, and almost every hand shot up. "Why?" asked Dr. Covey.

The answers were varied, and most were very altruistic. One student replied that he wanted to care for the poor. Another said she wanted to donate to schools. Yet another said he wanted to help forward the humanitarian efforts of his church.

Dr. Covey listened and complimented the students on their fine goals and desires. Then he stated simply, "If these are truly your desires, you will find a way to accomplish them now rather than later. If you wait until you are rich enough to do some good in the world, you will probably never do it." Those who know Dr. Covey know he certainly didn't wait.

Jon M. Huntsman, Sr., founder of Huntsman Chemicals, has been blessed with a great deal of wealth and is known worldwide for his philanthropic efforts. However, his generosity began long before he became wealthy. When Jon and his wife, Karen, were newlyweds, they lived on a small income. Karen kept track of the family finances and could always account for everything except $50 a month. She pointed the problem out to Jon, who wasn't overly concerned about it. Each month Karen tried to balance their tight little budget, and each month she wound up missing $50. The mystery was finally solved when a needy single mother at their church stood one day and said she would like to thank an anonymous donor who had been leaving $50 on her doorstep each month. Jon later explained, "If you cannot give when you have little, you will not be likely to give when you have everything" (see J. Michael Pinegar, "The Lord's Goods").

I admire Stephen R. Covey and Jon M. Huntsman, Sr., not just because of their philanthropy, but also because of their sense of urgency. They both felt—and responded to—the need to help others long before they had achieved professional and economic success. They were building others long before there were buildings named after them.

Satan has convinced many in the world that there is no God. He has convinced others there is no truth. But even believers are no better off if we allow him to convince us there is no hurry. We need to feel the urgency of drawing near to God and living in accordance with His truth. When the shepherds heard about the birth of the Lord, they went "with haste" (Luke 2:16) to find Him. They did not say, "Tomorrow or next week will be soon enough." We would do well to follow their example as we seek to serve Him.

> *Satan has convinced many in the world that there is no God. He has convinced others there is no truth. But even believers are no better off if we allow him to convince us there is no hurry.*

A SENSE OF MISSION

My family moved back to the United States from Africa when I was eight. My father returned to his university work, and my mother began teaching second grade. My brothers and I were often drafted to help set up her classroom. When the teachers at the elementary school I attended discovered I knew how to create a nice bulletin board, they sought my services as well. I think I was the only kid in the history of the world who had a file of bulletin board ideas! That may have been my first clue that I was headed toward a career in education.

When I was a university student and declared elementary education as my major, some of my buddies from high school thought I was crazy. They reminded me I could make more money in a different field, but I explained that I liked working with kids, and to me making money was less important than making a difference. That strong sense of mission moved me forward despite my friends' disapproval.

After graduating and beginning my career teaching sixth grade, I quickly learned that my friends had been right about the low pay. I also discovered that working with kids had some downs along with the ups. Still, I persevered because I knew I was making a difference. That sense of mission kept me going despite the realities I faced.

Now I am middle-aged, and I am still teaching—kids and the adults who teach them. Some of the friends who thought my choice of major was strange are now having midlife crises. They are not content with their big houses and fast cars. They are scrambling to change careers because they feel their lives lack significance. I haven't had a midlife crisis. I don't have time for one! I'm too busy trying to make a difference. That sense of mission has provided a deep and fulfilling abundance of significance.

You don't have to major in elementary education or be a schoolteacher to make a difference. Regardless of the majors we select or the jobs we have, we can all choose to live with a sense of mission by choosing to do right, even when it means taking a harder road. "Let your light so shine before men, that they may see your good works, and glorify your Father which is in heaven" (Matthew 5:16).

A SENSE OF INTEGRITY

A friend of mine who is an admirer of Martin Luther King was quite upset when she found out that during preparations for the fiftieth anniversary of his "I Have a Dream" speech, the National Park Service was spending hundreds of thousands of dollars to remove a quote from the King Memorial: "I was a drum major for justice, peace, and righteousness" (John A. Murray, "Where's God?" 10-A). Some say the words were misquoted and the paraphrase made Dr. King appear arrogant. Others say the quote had to go because it was offensive in today's world. If that is the case, I wonder which of Dr. King's words is now so offensive that it must be removed at such great cost. Is it *drum major?* Is it *righteousness?* Either way, I wonder how Reverend King would feel about the fact that not one of the fourteen quotes chosen for his memorial makes any mention of the Almighty.

Most of us will never have monuments raised to our memories in this lifetime, but if we did, what words would we want to have engraved on them? I would be happy to see "justice, peace, and righteousness" in bold letters on mine.

More important, I want those words engraved on my heart and my life, which can happen only as I choose to live with a sense of integrity.

Integrity is connected to justice because it acknowledges that good and evil exist independent of popular votes and opinion polls. Some say, "Wrath, greed, envy, sloth, pride, gluttony, and lust are neither bad nor good. They're only what you perceive them to be" (Paul Yensing Yee, "No Laughing Matter?" 8). But as real as our distinctive viewpoints may be, they do not alter God's view. We would be better off trying to live by God's truth instead of trying to redefine it.

We would be better off trying to live by God's truth instead of trying to redefine it.

Speaker and author Dan Clark wrote about being a guest on a live television talk show in which the hostess took issue with some of the values he promotes. She commented, "Who said your values are the right ones? Who put you in charge of telling us what is right?"

Dan Clark responded, "For some reason, many equate values with religion and immediately get their knickers in a twist." He went on to explain that some values such as charity, forgiveness, honesty, love, hard work, service, and excellence not only are integral to most religions but are "true and right—period" ("The Team and the Trophy," 129–30). Integrity demands that we humbly strive to follow true principles instead of arrogantly trying to consider ourselves the exceptions. Justice demands that no one is above God's law, no matter how entitled he or she may feel.

Along with justice, integrity is connected to peace. There can be no peace if we are living double standards—one way on Sunday and another on Monday, one way in public and another in private, one way when we are being supervised and another when we are not. The word *peace* comes from the Latin word *pax,* which means an agreement. Warring countries enjoy peace when they agree to stop fighting. We enjoy peace when our actions agree with our values.

Have you ever seen clips of people being filmed by a hidden camera? Sometimes it is pretty funny to see what they do when they think no one is watching. Other times it is shocking and downright sad. It is always quite revealing. I love a YouTube video that shows children who were filmed during the Stanford Marshmallow Experiment on delayed gratification. Each was placed in a room with a marshmallow on the table in front of him or her. Instructions were given that if the child could resist eating the marshmallow for fifteen minutes, he or she would receive an additional marshmallow. One by one the children were then left "alone" in a room, unaware that a hidden camera was recording everything. Some children immediately stuffed the marshmallow in their mouths. Others lasted a few minutes and then succumbed. Some tried to eat just a little bit off the bottom and then turned the marshmallow over so no one would know. A few patiently waited and received the promised reward. When I viewed some of these clips, I smiled at the children's responses, but I also wondered how I would have responded myself.

How would our actions be affected if we suddenly found out we were being filmed with a hidden camera? Would being filmed affect the way we drive or the way we respond when others cut us off in traffic? Would it affect what we choose to watch, read, or listen to for entertainment? Would it affect what images we view on the Internet? How about the tone of our conversations with others or what we say about others when they are not present? If the contents of our emails, texts, or Instagrams were made available to everyone—not just those to whom they were addressed—would we want to think again about what we have written or displayed?

Integrity fears no hidden cameras. The actions that count the most in life are those seen by the fewest people. We feel peace when we know that the size of our audience makes no difference to the quality of our performance. The everyday Christian acts seen only by Christ are usually the ones that make us most like Him.

Along with justice and peace, integrity is also connected with righteousness because it has to do with our motives as well as our behavior.

> *Integrity fears no hidden cameras. The actions that count the most in life are those seen by the fewest people.*

Righteousness is not just about doing the right thing but about doing it for the right reason.

When my wife and I were once traveling in Japan, we were overwhelmed trying to read the train schedules and make our way around the busy, crowded stations. At one particular stop, our connection was very tight. We had only a few minutes to make it to our next train and no idea how to ask anyone for help in Japanese. As we stood to leave our train car, I saw a man, woman, and child also stand and start gathering their bags. I approached the man, held out my ticket, pointed to our next destination, and then just shrugged helplessly. He smiled at me and my wife and then turned and carried on a little conversation with his family in Japanese. He then turned back to me and with another encouraging smile motioned for us to follow them—and follow them we did! We have never stayed as close to total strangers in our lives! They maneuvered us through the crowds and turnstiles, up and down the stairs, and got us to our train just as it was ready to pull out. We quickly said thank you in English, Japanese, and every other language we could think of. The man and his family smiled, bowed, and waved to us as our train left the busy station.

In our moment of need, we deeply appreciated this family's help, but we also appreciated their pure motives. They certainly didn't have to care about a couple of foreigners they would never see again. They expected and received no money. They didn't seem to be helping us out of duty or obligation; I saw no rolled eyes or exasperated expressions on their faces. All three of them were sincerely kind and gracious. They left us with the impression that they were happy to help.

As my wife and I put away our bags and settled in for the next leg of our journey, we realized we hadn't even had time to ask their names. We didn't know if helping us had been convenient for them. Perhaps they had had their own tight connection. They could have ignored my silent plea or simply pointed us in the right direction and called it good. Instead, they personally led us through a terminal that seemed like a maze to us. As I reflected on how much I appreciated the goodness of this family, all I could do was vow that I would strive to improve my own actions and motives.

In Psalm 139:23 we read, "Search me, O God, and know my heart; try me, and know my thoughts." It seemed to me, based on my short experience with this Japanese family, that they may have been up to such an examination. Integrity demands righteousness, and righteousness demands that we continually educate and elevate our desires and motives.

As an eighteen-year-old I won *Guideposts'* youth writing contest and had my story published in the magazine. Few remember or care. However, in all the years since that experience, I have been trying to live with greater consistency between my choices and values, and that's the story that really matters. My high school story required a few hours on a weekend and a mom who was willing to fix my misspelled words and punctuation mistakes. The story of my life has required much more. I have had to develop a sense of urgency, mission, and integrity that I did not always feel in high school.

Even now, some days are better than others. Sometimes I experience success, and sometimes I stumble and fail, but I continue to try—not because a teacher is forcing me, but because in addition to bringing me personal peace and chances to have a positive impact on others, my choosing to live as a daily disciple has opened the door for tremendous personal development. The real prize is not merely a scholarship, but all I am learning as I strive 7 days a week to allow the Savior to make me more like Him.

CHAPTER THREE

NEVER CHECK YOUR RELIGION AT THE DOOR

We've all seen sports fans lose control. People who are ordinarily kind and thoughtful can quickly become animals. They scream, swear, and hurl insults at referees and fans from the opposing team without giving their actions a second thought. They make obscene gestures at the players—even those on their own teams.

One father took his young son to a basketball game that ended up being a real nail-biter. The score was tied with only a few minutes remaining. The noise in the stands seemed about to lift the roof off the building. The father looked over to see if his son was enjoying the excitement and found him looking in the opposite direction. The dad said, "Son, the game is down there. You're missing all the action!"

"Oh, no, I'm not," the son responded. "That lady's eyes are about to bulge right out of her head, and when she yells her spit flies everywhere!"

What happened to "Do unto others as you would have others do unto you" (see Matthew 7:12)? What happened to "Blessed are the peacemakers" (Matthew 5:9)? There is nothing wrong with getting pumped up at a ball game, but fans can too easily cross the line between passion and stupidity.

After one such moment, a young basketball fan tried to excuse his degrading behavior at a game by saying, "We pay good money to see these games. We can act the way we want. We check our religion at the door" (R. Scott Lloyd, "Live Gospel in Small Ways"). This raises an interesting question: Is it *ever* appropriate to check our religion at the door? Do we dare to separate ourselves, ever, from the source of our strength?

There may be a necessary line between church and state, but there should never be a line between God and us!

I was once invited to speak at a conference in New York. One of the other presenters had titled his workshop "From Down and Out to Up and At 'Em." However, the program was printed with a typo: "From Down and Out to Up and Adam." The mistake may be better than the original title. Adam and Eve were down and out, but they got up and at 'em. When they left the Garden of Eden and entered the world, they did not check their religion at the border. God

> *There may be a necessary line between church and state, but there should never be a line between God and us!*

35

helped them by offering three gifts: protection, prayer, and promises. We have been given the same gifts.

PROTECTION

The first gift of God was protection. When Adam and Eve were found naked in the Garden of Eden, the Lord made "coats of skins, and clothed them" (Genesis 3:21). In addition to physical protection, the coats of skins offered spiritual protection. An animal had to be sacrificed—a powerful foreshadowing of the Savior's ultimate sacrifice. In this way the coats of skins became shields of love.

In J. K. Rowling's novel *Harry Potter and the Sorcerer's Stone,* young Harry learns the hidden secret of his mother's death when he was an infant, which is the reason evil ones recoil from him. Harry's school headmaster, Professor Dumbledore, explains:

"Your mother died to save you. If there is one thing Voldemort [the evil one] cannot understand, it is love. He didn't realize that love as powerful as your mother's for you leaves its own mark. . . . To have been loved so deeply, even though the person who loved us is gone, will give us some protection forever. It is in your very skin. Quirrell, full of hatred, greed, and ambition, sharing his soul with Voldemort, could not touch you for this reason. It was agony to touch a person marked by something so good" (299).

In writing about the coats of skins given to Adam and Eve, Wendy Ulrich explained that along with covering them literally, the skins also covered them symbolically: "The coat of skins seems to represent the soul-identity closest to our heart, shining with the lingering touch of God's deep and abiding love" ("Not Ashamed," 114). The Savior gave His life for us. To have been loved so deeply gives us protection forever.

PRAYER

The second gift Adam and Eve took with them from the garden into the world was prayer. In the garden they had been close to God. Can we even begin to understand the homesick yearning that must have filled their hearts when they were cast out? They and their posterity offered sacrifices, which included prayer (see Genesis 4). Adam and Eve knew God had heard them in the garden, but was He listening now that they were in the world?

Many in the world have wondered the same thing. *Les Misérables,* a French historical novel by Victor Hugo, tells the story of Jean Valjean, a peasant who is imprisoned for stealing bread to feed his sister's family. When he is finally released, he faces only rejection until a priest helps him. From then on Valjean spends his life helping others, which includes promising a dying woman he will seek out and care for her daughter, Cosette. True to his promise, he finds the child and raises her as his own. Cosette falls in love with Marius, a revolutionary student who is helping to instigate an uprising. In the heat of battle, Jean Valjean finds the young man injured and unconscious and saves Marius by carrying him through the sewers of Paris. It is there—not just in the world, but in the sewers of the world—that Valjean reaches upward in prayer. In the musical based on the novel, Jean Valjean prays and asks God to bring Marius safely home.

When I hear the song "Bring Him Home," I not only hear Jean Valjean singing about Marius, but I imagine the Savior singing about each of us. He descended below all things to save us. His sacrifice allows us the opportunity to go Home.

Prayers are not just the stuff of novels and theater productions. They can be a daily part of each of our lives. My daughter Wendee was helping her husband, Gian, set up his classroom in preparation for a new school year. Their two-year-old son, Roman, was with them and running out of patience quickly. Wendee finally told Gian she was going to take their toddler to the playground outside while he finished his inventory lists.

Roman loved going up and down the slide, but suddenly it started to rain. Wendee hurried to the door of the building and was discouraged to find it locked. She wanted to go tap on Gian's classroom window, but it was on the other side of the school, beyond the tall chain-link fence that surrounded the playground. She knew eventually Gian would come to find them, but Wendee didn't want to be out in the rain with an upset Roman. She said a quick prayer in her mind that Gian would come open the door. He never came.

With great effort, Wendee scaled the fence, leaving a

crying son wondering where his mom was going. She hurried to the other side of the building and knocked on Gian's window. Soon the family was all together inside. When Wendee told Gian about what had happened and how she had prayed, he said, "I actually had the strongest impression I should come to the playground and check on you, but I stayed to finish this last page. I'm sorry I didn't follow that prompting."

Wendee wasn't upset. She actually felt tremendous relief wash over her. God had answered her simple petition. Gian hadn't followed the impression he had received, but he had received it. God was aware of this young mother and her upset child stranded on the playground in the rain. It was a small thing—seemingly unimportant in the grand scheme of things. Still, it was a moment when once again Wendee was reminded that she is never alone. None of us are. Wendee's prayer didn't change the situation, but recognizing God's closeness to her filled her heart with gratitude.

My friend Virginia H. Pearce wrote, "The miracle of prayer doesn't reside in the ability to manipulate situations and events, but in the miracle of creating a relationship with God. Think about that carefully, would you? What does it do for you to have an assurance that the Lord is with you?" (*A Year of Powerful Prayer*, 186–87).

PROMISES

Along with protection and prayer, Adam and Eve discovered another gift—promises. In the garden they hid themselves because they were ashamed (see Genesis 3:10). They had yielded to Satan's temptations and broken a commandment, and consequently they would be cast out. However, it is never too late to make promises to obey, rebuild trust, and begin again. Only as we feel the strength of Satan's temptations do we recognize how powerful our simple promises to obey God can be.

Only as we feel the strength of Satan's temptations do we recognize how powerful our simple promises to obey God can be.

In J. R. R. Tolkien's trilogy *The Lord of the Rings,* a little hobbit named Frodo becomes the hope of the world when he is entrusted with the task of carrying an evil ring to the mountain where it can be destroyed. Obstacles loom on every side; some who have sworn to protect him prove themselves to be untrustworthy. At one point Frodo decides to set off on his own. He even determines to leave his best friend, Sam—but Sam, unlike others, understands the power of a promise.

In Peter Jackson's film adaptation of the first book of the trilogy, *The Fellowship of the Ring,* Frodo sets off in a boat alone. Although Sam can't swim, he plunges into the river to follow his friend. Frodo calls, "Go back, Sam. I'm going to Mordor alone."

Sam doesn't slow in the least as he says, "Of course you are. And I'm coming with you."

Realizing that nothing he says is going to change Sam's mind, Frodo reaches out and brings his drowning friend into the boat, at which point Sam says, "I made a promise, Mr. Frodo. A promise. 'Don't you leave him, Samwise Gamgee.' And I don't mean to. I don't mean to."

As we promise to obey God, it is like feeling God reach out to bring a drowning friend into His boat. We can't complete our life's journey alone, but we can do anything when we are hand in hand with God (see Matthew 19:26).

STANDING FOR JESUS

When Adam and Eve left the Garden of Eden, they could have checked their religion at the border. They could have left God behind. But instead, they realized how much they needed Him. Three gifts from heaven helped them in the world: protection, prayer, and promises. May we use these same gifts that blessed our first parents.

One person who knew the importance of those gifts was Ryan Rotela, who in 2013 was a junior at Florida Atlantic University. In an intercultural communications course, he and his classmates were told to write the name *Jesus* on a paper. Ryan did so. The instructor gave the students a brief time for reflection and then told class members to place the paper on the floor and stand up. Again Ryan complied. Next the instructor told class members to stomp on the paper bearing Jesus' name. Ryan refused. Instead, he picked up the paper and placed it on his desk. He explained to the instructor that, with all due respect, he felt the assignment was inappropriate and unprofessional. He said what he had been told to do was deeply offensive to him.

When Ryan later reported the incident to the instructor's superior, instead of receiving an apology, he was suspended from the university for not participating in the assignment. He was actually charged with violating the student code of conduct. Instead of reprimanding the instructor for giving such an assignment, university leaders brought academic charges against Ryan, who was summoned to report for a "student conduct conference" ("College Student Suspended for Refusing to STOMP on Jesus Sign").

After the incident was reported on local and national news, university officials changed their position. The director of media relations at the university issued an apology, stating that although the university environment embraces open discourse, this particular exercise was "insensitive and hurtful." The school agreed to expunge all academic charges from Ryan's student records and not take any further action against him.

The governor of the state of Florida applauded Ryan for "having the courage to stand up for his faith." In a written statement, the governor said, "It took great conviction and bravery to stand up and say what he was asked to do was wrong, and went against what he believed in" ("Florida School Apologizes"). I agree with the governor. Ryan faced great opposition, but instead of stomping on Jesus, Ryan stood up for Jesus. Who knows what lesson the instructor was trying to teach in his international communications course? Whatever it was, it was totally eclipsed by the lesson Ryan Rotela taught his instructor, classmates, and all of us.

Not long ago I spoke with Ryan personally about what happened and thanked him for refusing to demean the name of the Lord. He said that he actually had to make that decision twice: first when he was told to stomp on the sacred name written on his paper and second when he determined to go to an administrator about the incident. "The first one wasn't difficult," he said. "That just came naturally and spontaneously. The second choice was harder." Ryan had expressed his concerns to the instructor, and the instructor had ignored him, as if his opinion didn't matter at all. Ryan said, "I sat there in class wondering if I should let it go or if I should report the incident." Ryan didn't want to do anything without thinking it through. He certainly didn't want to cause problems for the instructor, but he did not want him to continue to do something so offensive in other classes. Ryan said, "I was feeling torn. I mean, I was sitting there trying to sort out what had just happened and how best to handle the situation. I kept asking myself, 'Am I just taking this too seriously? Am I making a big deal out of nothing? Am I the only one who felt the instructor went too far?'"

Surely there were other Christian students in that classroom. What was going through their heads? Maybe it was, "It doesn't matter what the teacher did. Just shut up and don't make waves." Maybe it was, "Don't be so rigid. You should be more tolerant and open-minded." Maybe it was something like, "We pay good money to take these classes. We can act the way we want. We check our religion at the door."

When I asked Ryan about that, he said he couldn't presume to speak for others. "All I know," he said, "is that there was only one girl—a tall girl—who came up right after class and said, 'Thanks for doing what you did.'" Ryan explained, "She gave me the reassurance that I wasn't alone. That's when I decided to go to the administrator, and then everything played out from there."

Was Ryan simply seeking attention? Did he want praise or notoriety? No, Ryan didn't foresee all that would occur: the reaction of the administration, the academic charges to be brought against him, the media attention, and the churches that united and organized marches to show their support. Ryan expressed appreciation for all who helped, but he admitted it was pretty overwhelming to a college student who would rather be out playing basketball with some of his buddies. "Anyone who is doing something like this to seek fame is never going to be able to hold up when the fame hits," Ryan assured. "Your reasons have to go deeper than that."

Did Ryan feel protected during his experience? "Yes," Ryan said. "When you stand up for what's right, you always have God on your side." Did Ryan find help in prayer? He said, "I've studied both Eastern and Western philosophies and religions, and one thing they all have in common is that they believe in a higher power and that we can communicate with Him. Prayer always helps." Did promises he had made to God make a difference for Ryan? He explained, "Hey, I didn't decide to stand up for Jesus when I was in that classroom. I decided much earlier. That's why it was so natural when the moment came. I was just living a commitment I had made earlier."

After the incident at Florida Atlantic University, Ryan's lawyer said, "Decades ago the Supreme Court ruled that students do not leave their First Amendment rights at the schoolhouse gate . . . [and] that is still true today" ("Student suspended"). It certainly was true for Ryan Rotela, who refuses to check his religion at the door—the schoolhouse door or any other.

What's next for Ryan? He said: "I'm going to keep trying to stand up for my morals in a world where that is getting harder and harder. There will be many more rallying calls like this one. Everyone is going to have to decide what he or she stands for." Ryan is right about that. The line between church and state has become a rope in a tug-of-war. There will be lawsuits and televised public marches and press conferences, but what matters most will always be the personal victories like Ryan's—not just on Sunday, but every day.

CHAPTER FOUR

WITHOUT WAX

When I was first learning Spanish, my teacher taught our class the word for *sincere.* In Spanish the word is made up of two smaller words: *sin,* which means "without," and *cera,* which means "wax." *Sincere:* "without wax." That certainly seemed like an odd combination of words. When I asked my teacher about it, he explained that the word *sincere* comes from the Latin *sincerus,* meaning "clean, pure, and sound." He then shared an often-repeated folk explanation about the word's beginnings. He said that long ago, dishonest sculptors who made items out of marble would cover any flaws or mistakes with wax. Then they would take their work to the market and sell it. The new owners would feel good about their purchases until they took them home and the hot sun melted the wax and exposed the flawed items for what they really were. Buyers got smart and began to ask, "Is this made without wax?" They wanted to know what they were getting. They didn't want something that looked wonderful on the outside but would not hold up in the heat of the sun, so the question became "Is this sincere?"

Those who claim to be Christians must live lives that are sincere—clean, pure, sound—the same on the inside as they appear on the outside. People should be able to trust that they will see Christ's image in our countenances and His teachings in our lives—not just on Sunday, but throughout the heat and pressure of a 7-day week. Living sincerely is difficult, but it is doable when we remember our sculptor is not a dishonest artisan but the perfect Creator. Christ is not just working on us but with us and through us. He condemned hypocrisy when He said, "Woe unto you, scribes and Pharisees, hypocrites! for ye make clean the outside of the cup and of the platter, but within they are full of extortion and excess" (Matthew 23:25). Christ helps us move beyond external appearances by going beyond self-acceptance, beyond relying on our own power, beyond preoccupation with ourselves. As we do, we are able to influence others in ways that go far beyond our wildest expectations.

> *Christ is not just working on us but with us and through us.*

BEYOND SELF-ACCEPTANCE

Living without wax goes beyond our willingness to reveal and accept our imperfections; it means that we are sincerely trying to correct them. Our goal is not to hide our flaws and try to look better, but to actually *become* better.

We live in a world that seems to admire "being yourself" more than improving yourself. Consider just a few of the bumper stickers and T-shirt slogans I have seen in recent years:

DON'T CHANGE

BEAUTIFUL MEANS TO BE YOURSELF

DON'T HIDE THE MADNESS

YOU ARE WHAT YOU ARE

ACCEPT YOURSELF

These slogans sound like pretty good advice on the surface—especially as we try to fight the tendency to compare ourselves to and compete with others. We all know people whose self-esteem has sunk to rock bottom because they have allowed the opinions of others to carry too much weight.

But if we look a little below the surface, this kind of advice isn't always as helpful as some may think. Despite all the bumper stickers and T-shirts that have been printed and sold, some of the most miserable people I know are the ones who have accepted themselves just the way they are and refuse to change.

I once asked a rebellious teenager why he had chosen to cover himself with tattoos and piercings. He said, "I'm just being unique." Couldn't he see that what he called "being unique" was simply conforming to a current fad image? He didn't stand out; he blended in. Instead of leaving his mark on the world, this young man was letting the world leave its mark on him. Like this teen, too many are content with the message to "define yourself," when Christ's message was to "refine yourself" (see Matthew 5:48).

I agree with Eleanor Roosevelt, who said, "One's philosophy is not best expressed in words; it is expressed in the choices one makes. In the long run, we shape our lives, and we shape ourselves. . . . And the choices we make are ultimately our own responsibility" (*You Learn by Living*, foreword).

BEYOND OUR OWN POWER

Our task as Christians is not to be ourselves as much as it is to become more like the Savior. The question for 7-day Christians to consider may not simply be, "What would Jesus do?" but rather, "What would Jesus have *me* do?" Those who have the courage to find—and act on—such answers will surely experience the Savior's transforming power.

We do not do ourselves or anyone else any favors by pretending to be something we are not. Christ said, "For ye are

> *The question for 7-day Christians to consider may not simply be, "What would Jesus do?" but rather, "What would Jesus have* me *do?"*

like unto whited sepulchres, which indeed appear beautiful outward, but are within full of dead men's bones, and of all uncleanness" (Matthew 23:27). But we do not help ourselves or anyone else by sitting around and insisting that everyone accept us just the way we are: "Hey, I'm full of dead men's bones and uncleanness, so like it or lump it! It's just the way I am! Get over it!"

Those who claim they can't change are probably right. They can't change themselves, but Christ can transform those who seek Him in humility. We may be content to cover ourselves with wax and *look* good, but Jesus can help us *become* good. We must trust the Master Sculptor, who said, "As the clay is in the potter's hand, so are ye in mine hand" (Jeremiah 18:6).

I have a friend who said, "Brad, I prayed about it, and God told me He loves me just the way I am."

I said, "Of course He does. Just like I love my grandbabies just the way they are. But that doesn't mean I don't want them to learn to walk, talk, read, and write. Loving them as they are doesn't mean I don't want them to grow, develop, and reach their potential."

BEYOND OURSELVES

Well-meant pieces of advice to "be yourself," "accept yourself," and "love yourself" all have one thing in common: the word *self.* Jesus taught that the greatest love of all is not learning to love yourself but learning to love God and others (see Mark 12:30–31). He said, "He that findeth his life shall lose it: and he that loseth his life for my sake shall find it" (Matthew 10:39).

As we emulate the Savior, we are led to engage with others in the world even as we distance ourselves from worldliness. James wrote that pure and undefiled religion is "to visit the fatherless and widows in their affliction, and to keep [yourself] unspotted from the world" (James 1:27). About that charge, Terryl and Fiona Givens have written: "Kindness only exists when there is someone to whom we show kindness. Patience is only manifest when another calls it forth. So it is with mercy, generosity, and self-control. . . . Salvation was intended all along as a collaborative enterprise, though we often miss the point. The confusion is understandable, since our current generation's preference for 'spirituality' over 'religion' is often a sleight of hand that confuses true discipleship with self-absorption" (*The God Who Weeps*, 112–13).

> *Well-meant pieces of advice to "be yourself," "accept yourself," and "love yourself" all have one thing in common: the word* self. *Jesus taught that the greatest love of all is not learning to love yourself but learning to love God and others.*

True disciples are not self-absorbed, and God can use them to change the world—perhaps not all at once, but one heart at a time. This can set off a chain reaction. One person can help five friends, who then might feel motivated to help five more, and so on. It is not difficult to see that one can turn into five and then into 25 and then to 125. Let's keep going: 625 to 3,125 to 15,625 to 78,125 to 390,625. The influence of one person can ultimately reach billions.

Too unrealistic? Consider the life of Jesus Christ Himself. Dr. James Allan Francis once delivered a sermon entitled "Arise, Sir Knight!" in which he reminded us that Jesus was born in an obscure village to a peasant woman. He never owned property, wrote a bestseller, or held a political office, and He had no degrees or strings to pull. In fact, He never traveled more than a few hundred miles beyond the place of His birth, and yet He changed the world forever. Think of how powerfully and positively the world has been affected by that one life. Think how He continues to transform us all. It is through Jesus that all our ordinary lives can become extraordinary!

BEYOND EXPECTATIONS

Living sincerely—without wax—is important, but our ultimate goal can't be only that; even Hitler and Genghis Khan could have been called sincere in their wickedness. Our goal can't stop at changing the world; both Hitler and Genghis Khan did that. Our goal has to be to change the world for good, as Jesus did. As we emulate Christ, we can influence the world in ways that go beyond what we may ever expect or imagine.

On a short trip in which I was flying out to and back from my destination on the same day, I packed only a small carry-on bag. When it was time to board the flight home, the announcement came that the plane was delayed. The flight was finally canceled due to mechanical problems. This was the last flight out that night, so everyone was upset.

All the passengers headed to the help desk, where there was only one airline worker because of the late hour. I was as frustrated as everyone else as I took my place in the long line of tired travelers. The airline worker was trying her best, but soon people were screaming and swearing at her and at each other. Civility was totally forgotten. Perhaps if I had been heading out rather than home I might have felt a little more anxious, but I actually stayed calm for once. I felt thankful we hadn't boarded a faulty aircraft!

When my turn to be helped finally came, the frazzled airline worker rebooked my flight for the next morning and then handed me my new boarding pass and a voucher for a nearby hotel. "Thank you," I said sincerely. She looked up and stared at me in stunned silence. Perhaps she thought I was being sarcastic, but I just smiled and repeated, "Thank you." Her eyes actually moistened as she said, "No, sir, thank *you!*"

As I walked toward the airport exit to catch a shuttle to the hotel, I considered what had just happened and was grateful I had kept my cool. There have certainly been times when I haven't, and I regret them, but this time I had allowed Christ to work through me.

I approached the waiting area for the shuttle and noticed a young mother who had also been scheduled on the canceled flight trying to manage multiple suitcases and a crying baby at the same time. Without asking, I just stepped toward her and said, "Here, let me get those for you." I picked up the bags and asked where she needed to go. We were heading to the same hotel, so I volunteered to carry her luggage to the shuttle stop and on to the van.

We made conversation during the short drive, and then I helped again with her bags while she checked in. By now her baby had fallen asleep. It had been little trouble for me to help, since I had only a small carry-on. As I assisted the mother toward the elevator, she pulled me aside and whispered, "Are you an angel?"

She was speaking so quietly I didn't think I had heard her right, and I said, "Pardon?"

She asked again, a bit louder, "Are you an angel? You can tell me. I won't tell anyone. I promise."

Looking back, I have to laugh. Maybe this mom had watched one too many episodes of the television show *Touched by an Angel*. Maybe she had read one too many angel encounters on the Internet. Whatever the reason, she actually thought that I might be an angel.

"No," I answered with a smile as I helped her toward the elevator. "I'm just a disciple."

Are simple acts of service so rare in this world that people think they are limited to angels? I hope not. Are sincere and selfless expressions of gratitude so rare that they bring people to tears? I hope not.

When I decided to thank an airline worker instead of getting upset, I wasn't thinking of changing the world. And I was really surprised when the young mother I had helped was sure she had met an angel in disguise. I was merely trying to help out. Who knows what happened next? Did I start a chain reaction that reached around the world? Maybe I did or maybe I didn't. Either way, I felt the joy that accompanies small and simple acts of service. Whether or not my choices impacted the world, they allowed Christ to impact a few people through me, and this allowed me to take a few baby steps toward becoming like Him.

In Psalm 40:10 we read, "I have not hid thy righteousness within my heart; I have declared thy faithfulness and thy salvation: I have not concealed thy lovingkindness and thy truth from the great congregation." On some days that scripture can read like a statement of fact. Some days it serves as a reminder. Many days it reads as a distant goal. However far along I may feel in my discipleship, I must continue to strive to not hide righteousness within or conceal loving kindness. I can share these gifts with others as freely as God shares them with me. The results will always go beyond expectations.

Richard John Neuhaus wrote, "The kind of people we are is more important than what we can do to improve the world; indeed, being the kind of people we should and can be is the best, and sometimes the only, way to improve the world" ("C. S. Lewis in the Public Square," 30).

Learning the Spanish word for *sincere* opened my eyes not only to a new language but to a way of living. For many years now I have tried to face the world without wax. When the hot sun comes out and melts away all façades, I hope what is left is not "the real me" that others must "accept" because "it's just the way I am." Instead, I hope that others will see a little bit of Christ's light in my eyes and His image in my countenance. To me, living sincerely doesn't mean simply standing before others exposed, but exposing others to Christ's perfect example through my meager attempts to emulate Him. And who knows when one person I reach might set off a chain reaction that will stretch around the globe? If I live my beliefs every day, God can use even someone as ordinary as I am to change the world.

CHAPTER FIVE

TO BE LIKE
A CHILD

I have spent much of my life working with children and those who teach and care for them. I have noticed children quite naturally possess attributes that we sometimes end up missing in our adult lives: an inner desire to do right, a sense of worth, the ability to be happy, a capacity to love, an innate sense of wisdom, and a deep and trusting faith. It is as if children are carrying full buckets of water, and then they stagger into their teenage years and the water starts sloshing out. Then they face the blows of adulthood, and even more water escapes. Soon people are standing around with empty buckets. This emptiness is not because the buckets were never full; the buckets become empty when people lose what they once had (see Tom Rath and Donald O. Clifton, *How Full Is Your Bucket?*). As we strive to emulate the Savior and be true Christians 7 days a week, God refills our buckets, and we understand why Jesus said, "Verily I say unto you, Except ye be converted, and become as little children, ye shall not enter into the kingdom of heaven" (Matthew 18:3).

DESIRE TO DO RIGHT

Jennifer Eggleston, an elementary school principal, told me how she intervened when two first graders were fighting. She asked, "What's going on here?"

One boy pointed to the other and said, "He is not choosing the right!"

The other boy looked at Mrs. Eggleston and on the verge of tears said, "Tell me what to do and I'll choose the right. I want to choose the right!"

Think back to when your greatest desire was to choose the right. Think back to when the world seemed gentler, to the time when you brushed your teeth or looked both ways at street crossings because these were things your parents had taught you were right. Did you kneel by your bed to say prayers and just know that God had nothing more important to do in His vast universe than to listen to you?

Coming from a highly religious family, I was a child with a drive to do right, but by sixth grade I was beginning to grow up, becoming aware of what others thought, and realizing it wasn't always easy to choose the right. Water was already beginning to slosh out of my bucket.

That year we took turns being assigned to work lunch duty. We covered ourselves with large white aprons and wore little nets on our heads. We worked either serving or cleaning up. In my school the coveted job was passing out milk, and one day I got it! I was assigned along with another boy to distribute the little milk cartons. When we started to run low, I went back to the refrigeration locker to get a few more crates. I had just brought out a crate when a milk-passer-wannabe came up and said, "You're not strong enough to lift the milk! I'll lift the milk!" He pushed right by me and entered the refrigeration locker to get another crate. That's when I shut the door on him. I took my crate up to the serving line and kept passing out milk cartons and never told anyone! I guess someone heard the poor kid yelling and finally opened the door.

Indignation spills a lot of water out of our buckets. A better way of handling bullies did not occur to me.

But even as I made wrong choices, I still had a drive to do right. My sixth-grade teacher, Mr. Van Wagoner, was always pleasant, which made it even more memorable when he came into the classroom one day and threw his book down on the desk. Everybody in the class jumped, and he said, "You listen to me because I'm going to teach you something that is not in that book." He then said, "Self-pity is the worst disease." I don't even remember what had occurred that made him say that, but I've never forgotten his words. Throughout sixth grade and junior high, whenever times became hard and I was tempted to feel sorry for myself, I recalled Mr. Van Wagoner's words. What he said was right, and I didn't want to lose the drive to do right I had as a child.

SENSE OF WORTH

Another attribute missing from too many adult lives is a sense of worth. In Isaiah we read, "I will make a man more precious than fine gold" (13:12). Children feel golden! Every baby born thinks he or she is the center of the universe. Not a baby in this world waits to cry until he finds out if the cool babies are crying. No baby ever checks another baby's diapers to see if she is wearing the right brand name. Babies come into the world with full buckets.

> *Every baby born thinks he or she is the center of the universe. Not a baby in this world waits to cry until he finds out if the cool babies are crying.*

Young children possess a vibrant sense of their own value and potential. I was once teaching a group of primary-grade children a song about a famous figure in American history. The lyrics went something like this: "Who was the one who did this great thing? Who was the one who did that great thing?" And I asked the children, "Who *was* the one who did those great things?" A little boy named Matt raised his hand and announced to everyone, "It was *me!*" He believed it. At a young age, he knew he could do great things.

Children know they are important. My wife, Debi, worked part-time as a nurse in the same-day surgery unit at a local hospital. One day when she was outside eating lunch on a bench, a little boy rode up on his bike and said, "Hi! Do you remember me?"

My wife looked at the boy but had no recollection of meeting him. He saw her hesitation and asked with disappointment, "You don't remember *me?*"

Debi finally said, "I'm sorry. Where would I know you from?"

The child pointed to the hospital and announced, "I was born here!"

That little kid thought he was so important that every nurse in the hospital was going to remember the day he was born!

We're naturally going to lose some of that exhilaration, but many of us lose way too much too fast. Many of us start caring in unhealthy ways about what others think and say. Some people, struggling with fears and insecurities, try to replenish their own buckets by emptying ours. They ridicule and find fault, and we give their words too much credibility. A sense of worth can be drained from our buckets by thoughtless people even though what they take from us does not really add to their own supply. Soon our buckets are empty. The girl who used to twirl around in front of a mirror like a princess now greets the same mirror calling herself "Fat! Stupid! Unpopular! Ugly!"

Contrast those negative feelings with the mood of this

story written by one of my sixth graders, a boy named Brett who had not yet lost too much water from his bucket. He titled it "The Strong Day":

> "Pull out your journals," exclaimed Mr. Wilcox. It was another boring day in school. All of a sudden the walls started to shake and move toward the center of the room. Everyone scrambled to the door and some ran for the window. The ground was shaking hard and all the kids were screaming. A couple of the kids and I ran back into the school. "C'mon," I yelled, "Let's get these walls pushed back." Even Mr. Wilcox came in with his bulging muscles and helped push everything back to normal. The earthquake, however, was still shaking the ground. That is until Mr. Wilcox yelled at it and it never shook again. It never even thought of shaking! "Brett, my buddy," Mr. Wilcox called me in front of everyone. "You have saved the day. I'm so proud of you." His voice sounded like it was full of love. I'm so cool. I'm totally cool. I'm the coolest of the cool!

I hope you noticed the part about my "bulging muscles." I love that. How many adults imagine themselves stopping an earthquake and pushing falling walls back in place? How many think of themselves as the coolest of the cool? We need to remember the days when we truly felt capable, important, and of worth. It's time to allow God to refill our buckets.

ABILITY TO BE HAPPY

Another attribute children have is the ability to be happy. Children are naturally happy. I have seen children on almost every continent—many of whom have little in the way of worldly goods—and they always seem to have big smiles on their faces. These children don't wait for happiness. They create happiness.

In Psalm 128:1–2, we read a promise to "every one that feareth the Lord; that walketh in His ways": "Happy shalt thou be." We are not told that happiness depends on what we look like, what others think of us, or what material possessions we have. The promised happiness comes from our relationship with and obedience to the Lord. As adults we may foolishly think happiness comes from winning a competition, enjoying popularity, being blessed with good health, or having not experienced divorce or some form of abuse. Thus happiness may seem forever out of our reach. ("I'll be happy when I lose ten pounds," or "I'll be happy when I find a spouse," or "I'll be happy when I get a raise.") Children create their happiness by choosing to be happy now. For years my mom had a little plaque in her kitchen that read, "Happiness is a city in the state of mind." Regardless of the state, province, or nation in which they were born, children know the City of Happiness—it is their birthright.

Some children have experiences that can rob their buckets early. We must recognize their needs and help them learn ways to replenish their precious supply. In one class of sixth graders, I taught a deaf girl who was a quick learner and a gifted lip reader, but her happiness bucket was already half-empty. Being mainstreamed into a public school classroom for the first time was challenging her socially and academically. When it was time for lunch I always walked my students down the hall, and if we had to wait in a long line, I would sing little songs while we waited. You can imagine how that must have looked to a girl who could not hear.

After one such impromptu concert, when the rest of the class went into the lunchroom, this girl pulled me aside and said, "Mr. Wilcox, you are *always* happy! Don't you have any problems?"

That was the moment for which I had waited. I knelt down to be right at her eye level, and I said, "Watch my lips. Don't take your eyes off my lips. Yes. I have problems, but you can have problems and be happy at the same time." I don't think anyone had ever told her that. It made a difference to her. That perspective can make a difference to us, too.

CAPACITY TO LOVE

One first grader sought out his principal because he was concerned about a friend. In his best grown-up voice he explained, "Mrs. Eggleston, Pablo is in love. He has fallen way, way down in love and we need to help him!"

Little children can desire to do right, recognize their

worth, and create their own happiness; a reason they can do this is that they also have their buckets full of love. Most children readily accept and give open, spontaneous, unconditional love. The mothers who brought their children to Jesus for a blessing must have recognized this quality in their little ones and in the Savior. But the Apostles, who were still learning, did not, and attempted to send them away. However, Jesus welcomed the children, saying, "for of such is the kingdom of God" (Luke 18:16).

As much as we think we are loving the children in our lives, they are actually loving us even more. It's phenomenal to see how freely children share their hearts. I experienced this quite literally with a student in my sixth-grade classroom. James had been born with a heart problem. He had had his first open-heart surgery when he was only in first grade, and during this sixth-grade year he had to be scheduled for another. On the day he received this news, he was quite discouraged. This boy who usually filled our classroom with enthusiastic chatter was subdued. He dragged through the day, and I wanted to help him feel better. I wanted to build him up and lift his spirits.

When the final bell rang, I asked James to stay and help me put away some supplies, which gave us a chance to talk as we worked. I said, "James, your parents wrote me a note telling me about the surgery. What is going to happen?"

He replied, "They are going to open my chest, open up my heart, and then take out the valve that doesn't work and replace it with a pig valve."

I asked, "How do you feel about that?"

He said, "I think it's gross! I don't want a pig valve. I think that's sick. I want a bionic valve!"

"What happens if the pig valve doesn't work?"

"I guess they'll just take it out and put in another one. And if that doesn't work," he said matter-of-factly, "I guess I'll just die."

The empty classroom was silent. Neither James nor I spoke, but inside my head it was as if someone were screaming. I looked into the eyes of my young student and said, "Don't die, James. You can have my heart."

"No, Mr. Wilcox," he smiled—the first smile I'd seen all day. "I can't take your heart. You have a good heart. I love your heart."

I had wanted to lift James. I had wanted to help him and love him, but like the true child he was, he lifted me. He helped me. He loved me.

That's the kind of love we need to put back into our buckets. It is time to feel and express love as openly and as unconditionally as children do. "Thou shalt love thy neighbour as thyself" (Matthew 19:19), the Lord taught, and also, the "stranger that dwelleth with you . . . love him as thyself" (Leviticus 19:34). On the night before Jesus was crucified, He gave His disciples a "new commandment": "That ye love one another; as I have loved you, that ye also love one another. By this shall all men know that ye are my disciples, if ye have love one to another" (John 13:34–35).

SENSE OF WISDOM

Wisdom is another childlike attribute we adults need to find again. Children are wise. They haven't yet learned how to think in the same words and ways adults do; their wisdom is their own, and it reflects what they have learned from their own experiences. If you don't believe me, read the words of my young niece, who wrote the following: "If I were in charge of the world I'd cancel war, bullies and weirdoes. I would have more friends, peace, books, and airplanes would all be safe. If I were in charge, every person would eat his meals. Bad drugs would all be burned, and people would never be lonely."

Almost all of us used to think that clearly. Things were pretty straightforward—wrong or right. Then we moved into adolescent and finally adult years and allowed others to convince us that life is filled with gray areas. Unlike my niece, we started to think that bullying had to be tolerated. My niece's desire to "cancel" war got trumped by economic issues or upcoming elections.

Empty bucketers ignore the dangers of addictive substances and risky behaviors: "It's no big deal. Everyone is doing it. No one will know. Just once won't hurt." Pretty soon we find ourselves saying and doing things we would never have done when we were thinking a little more clearly.

As a young Cub Scout, my son demonstrated the wisdom of good sense and Christian teachings when he wrote the following about his duty to God:

Doing my duty to God means I have jobs to do for Jesus. Some of those jobs are

* Try to help more people to come to church.

* Go to church unless you're sick or something else.

* Don't say swear words even if a lot of your friends do.

* Don't do drugs even if someone says it's cool.

* Don't murder anyone or suicide yourself.

To me, that's what the scriptures mean when they tell of being "filled with the spirit of wisdom" (Exodus 28:3). It's time for us grown-ups to ask God to refill our buckets.

TRUSTING FAITH

Children do have an inner desire to do right, a natural sense of worth, the ability to be happy, a capacity to love, and an innate sense of wisdom, but their foundational and crowning attribute is a natural deep and trusting faith. How many of us have ever been running around panicked with a problem and had a young child remind us to pray about it? How many have been startled when a child is more upset that Jesus might not like what he has done than that Mom has sent him to his room? How many of us have heard a child pray for a friend or neighbor who is sick or troubled?

When children have been taught about God, their buckets are spontaneously filled with faith.

How much faith do we adults have in our faith buckets? Are we full, partly full, or totally empty?

Many adults may recognize that it has been a while since they have been as close to God as they should be. Perhaps they have settled for following rules instead of following the Savior. Perhaps they feel there have been too many hurts, mistakes, and regrets along the way. We all need to rediscover faith like that of our children.

Some intermediate-grade students were participating in a special writers' workshop. Because it was not sponsored by a public school, the instructor was free to invite the children to write on a variety of topics he would not have tackled in a typical classroom. One was, "If I met God." Here are some of the responses:

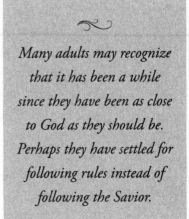

Many adults may recognize that it has been a while since they have been as close to God as they should be. Perhaps they have settled for following rules instead of following the Savior.

"If I met God He would be in the light. I couldn't see His face in detail. His voice would be soft and calm like flowing music. He would hug me and warm feelings would come over me."

"If I met God He would wipe my tears away. He would hold me in His arms."

"His voice would sound low, like a sound you never think of—like heaven and like you never want to leave."

"Sometimes I wonder if God really exists, but sometimes I feel His love around me. I mostly feel His love when I sing, pray, or hear the word *beautiful* because Jesus is beautiful."

These children did not imagine their experience with God using the words and images their parents would have chosen. Their words and images are wonderful because they are spontaneous and loving and from the heart. All the experiences these children associate with God emphasize His love, His warmth, and His very personal concern. All are expressions of childlike faith.

C. S. Lewis, sometimes called "the great Christian apologist," wrote a children's book series, *The Chronicles of Narnia,* with Christian-inspired characters and values. Aslan, the great lion, represents Christ, the king who rules with love and wisdom, submitting himself to abuse and death to save his friends.

Lewis expressed his ultimate trust in children's faith at the end of one of the later books, *Prince Caspian.* Susan, one of the children who has frequently visited Narnia, is too old to return again. She is unhappy that she will not be able to be with Aslan, but he tells her that he will always be with her—that he is in the other world as well. He explains that she has been brought to Narnia to get to know him so that she will be able to recognize him when she meets him outside. Through Aslan, children all over the world, of many backgrounds and denominations, have learned to recognize and respond to the individual love and concern, the noble and brave actions, and the infinite sacrifice of Jesus Christ. They do so naturally; their response to such stories contributes a little more to the faith already in the bucket.

Scriptures assure, "The just shall live by his faith" (Habakkuk 2:4). It's time to realize that God is real and He wants to be close to us if we will let Him. For every person who says belief is foolish, there are others who witness that there is a spiritual side of our natures that cannot be overlooked without serious consequences. For every person who says we can't change, there are others whose lives are evidence of Christ's transforming power. For every person who finds fault with organized religion, there are others who show with their words and actions that it is possible to find and live at a higher level. For every person who claims that faith is a weakness, there are others who testify that faith is the source of true inner strength.

In today's world, many people try to motivate positive changes by saying "Move forward! Press onward!" Instead, I say, "Look back!" This may sound like strange advice, but let us remember that Christ referred to His Apostles as "little children" (John 13:33). These

For every person who says we can't change, there are others whose lives are evidence of Christ's transforming power.

were grown men, yet He called them little children. As old as we may get, as grown up as we may appear, as sophisticated and knowledgeable as we may become, we are little children in His eyes. Each must choose to be like a child for Him.

CHAPTER SIX

FACING OUR PEOPLE FEARS

"What is your worst fear?" I once asked my children.

"Bees!" answered Wendee immediately. That was a predictable answer after her encounter with an unfriendly swarm at a neighborhood picnic a few years earlier. She had been stung more than twenty times.

Russell, who was in fifth grade at the time, admitted he was "a little" afraid of sharks. He had seen them only in movies, but that was close enough for him.

Four-year-old Whitney said, "Daddy, I don't like the big booms in the sky." Of course, she was describing thunder.

I turned to my youngest, David, and asked, "Are you afraid of anything?" His eyes got big and he nodded his head vigorously. "What is your worst fear?" I prodded.

He squared his little shoulders, stuck out his chin, put his hands on his hips, and declared, "Vacuums!"

As we mature, our fears shift and change. We may fear

greater pain than bee stings, incidents with human sharks, or emotional lightning and thunderstorms; and we may fear vacuums of the societal and economic (rather than the housekeeping) variety. Many of us put the effects of war, natural disasters, medical problems, and serious accidents, along with mental and spiritual challenges, at the top of our lists. But there are some childhood fears we don't outgrow. A high percentage of us continue to dread peer disapproval and humiliation. We might try to find more sophisticated labels for it, but essentially most of us fear being alone and being ridiculed, and I don't see many adults standing in line to be embarrassed in front of others.

FEARS WE DON'T OUTGROW

My colleague John Hilton III and I asked several adults to tell us how the fear of what others will think or do might apply to them. Consider some of their responses:

• "Isn't the most obvious adult experience of peer pressure expressed in our downright skittishness about sharing our religious beliefs and opinions? We're so afraid of others' reactions that we won't speak up."

• "As I got older and was still dating, I ran into a lot of peer pressure from would-be suitors. One day I said to myself, 'I cannot believe I am thirty-plus years old, and I am feeling peer pressure to conform!'"

- "We have children who are very involved in sports. The adult peer pressure to act a certain way, cheer a certain way, dress a certain way, and backbite each other as parents or families has been enormous!"

- "In the past, when I was working, and now, as I watch my husband's business demands, I see the business world includes a lot of peer pressure regarding expectations and competition that are very similar to what we experienced in our teenage years."

- "I think there is a great deal of peer pressure in material things, such as 'Do I have a nice enough car and house so the neighbors don't look down on me?' 'Do I go on enough vacations not to feel like a loser?' 'Am I wearing the right clothes?'"

As adults we may be more successful in hiding our insecurities and masking our self-doubts than our kids are, but for many of us, "people fears" are still there. Perhaps we have missed an important message in the scriptures: When an angel appeared to Zacharias in the temple, he said, "Fear not" (Luke 1:13). When an angel came to Mary, he said, "Fear not" (Luke 1:30). When an angel appeared to the shepherds, he said, "Fear not" (Luke 2:10). When John saw the risen Lord, he was told, "Fear not" (Revelation 1:17). Negative community reactions to unexpected pregnancies or sudden flock abandonment were not to be feared, nor were the supernatural light and heavenly visitations. The messages and instructions were more important than social or circumstantial fears. After nine months of enforced silence, Zacharias learned to step past his fears and insist that his son be named John, despite the disapproval of the crowd. How can we avoid fearing how our actions or behavior might be misinterpreted, mocked, and otherwise punished by others? Following are a few ways that have been helpful to me.

EXPECTING THE BEST

We tend to be pessimists in our expectations of how others will judge us when we don't measure up to someone's proclaimed standards. Recall that one of the respondents to the survey said she felt the parents of her children's teammates watching the way she dressed, behaved, and cheered. My experience has shown, however, that others usually aren't paying as much attention to us as we think they are. Most people are simply too worried about themselves to spend much time analyzing us. We may worry about whether our hair is in place, our clothes are just right, and our comments are clear. But those around us are usually so worried about their own hair, clothes, and comments that they're not even noticing us.

I learned an important lesson about the fear of being watched as I struggled with my brief and limited sports career. Growing up in Africa did not prepare me for the sports-saturated culture I encountered when I returned to the United States. I had not learned to play football, basketball, or baseball, and suddenly I was supposed to know all the rules and was expected to play well. When other children found out I didn't play—or even know how to—I was always picked last for any team. No one wanted to lose because of me, and I didn't want to lose because of me either. All too soon I was caught in the downward cycle

My experience has shown that others usually aren't paying as much attention to us as we think they are. Most people are simply too worried about themselves to spend much time analyzing us.

of avoiding sports because I was not good at them and never getting better because I never played. A boy with no basket-shooting skills suffers in elementary school and agonizes in junior high. By high school I solved the problem by becoming the school mascot and cheering for others from inside a bulldog costume. Any foolishness would be blamed on the bulldog, not on me.

As an adult, I became too busy to worry much about sports. Then one day I was informed that I had been elected by the student body at my university to be part of a faculty basketball team. It was Disability Awareness Week, and we were supposed to play against a team of wheelchair athletes to raise money for charity.

I was terrified. I tried everything to get out of the obligation, but everyone kept telling me what an honor it was to have been selected to participate. Apparently, no one had told the student body that I wasn't supposed to get picked for teams. The game day drew closer, and I was almost sick with nerves. This time I would not be hiding on the sidelines behind the big foam head of the bulldog. I would be on the court, where everyone could see. What would they think? What would they say?

The big day finally arrived. The faculty team was warming up on one side of the court and the wheelchair athletes on the other. I worried whether I was dribbling and shooting right. My insides were in such a knot I could hardly move. Then I looked out at the large crowd that had gathered to watch the game and realized that not one person was looking in my direction. Every spectator was being amazed and entertained by the incredible skills of the wheelchair athletes. These players were meant to be the focus of attention. I was part of the backdrop to help them look good, and suddenly that didn't feel bad at all.

What a freeing moment it was to realize that the fans couldn't care less about me! Suddenly I was no longer frozen by what they might think or what they might say. I didn't magically turn into a basketball star, but I did relax. I finally did something I had never before done as a child or teen: I had fun playing a sport. Freed from the weight of seeking others' approval, I could expect the best from the experience. I was glad I hadn't let my people fears keep me from participating. My investment in mental anguish and continual worry was wasted, but fortunately, the loss was reversible.

HEARING THE "HIDDEN MESSAGE"

Perhaps some are thinking, "Well, maybe no one watched or laughed at you, but people always watch and laugh at me." Many have such fears because in the past someone has laughed at their awkwardness. We must try to expect the best and realize that most people aren't going to tease or belittle, but some individuals do enjoy causing pain and embarrassment. They attempt to hide their own inadequacies behind insulting and embarrassing others. When cruel individuals start to make their snide comments, we need to listen for the hidden message—not just the obvious message coming out of their mouths, but the less obvious message behind those words.

We've all seen people giving speeches who looked so frightened we wanted to dial 911 before they fell over dead. Yet those same speakers usually began their talks with something like "I'm so happy to be here" or "I'm thankful for this opportunity." On such occasions, the surface message spoken is an attempt to hide the individual's true feelings, and it is not convincing.

Similarly, individuals who ridicule or exclude others are using words or social manipulation to cover a hidden message—usually that they don't feel good about themselves. If someone can make others laugh at my clumsiness, the group might be less likely to notice his problem. Some people exclude others as a way of building their own public images.

It's surprising how loudly and continually some people yell to cover up the fact that they have nothing worthwhile to say. We need to see through their attempts. I've learned those who don't think much of me usually think even less of themselves.

In middle school, a young girl who was gifted in mathematics speedily turned over her papers the moment they were returned for fear the boys would mock and tease her for being a "brain" if they should glimpse her high scores. As she became more mature, she realized that although she would not "show off" her scores, she did not need to feel sick with fear that someone might see them. Her real friends respected her abilities; those who mocked her might well have teased because they knew they could not have done as well. If they mocked loudly enough, no one would be likely to ask about their scores. Recognizing the hidden message, she was able to relax and enjoy her advanced mathematics class. If a middle-school student can do it, so can we.

When adults behave as if they were still in middle school and gossip behind our backs or dish out "humorous" cutting remarks and rude comments in public, hearing the hidden message behind them can soften the blows, help us keep perspective, and give us reasons to stay positive.

Acting with Confidence

If we are confident in our principles, standards, faith, and actions, we do not need to fear the rejection or ridicule of those who do not share them. People may be tempted to lie when the truth might bring embarrassment. Some may spend more than they can afford if they feel they will be disparaged for not having the right brands or styles of clothes. Some may pretend to have education or experiences that they think may impress others or enhance their social position. But when we know that what we are doing is right, we can have confidence in holding our heads up and resisting the lie, living within our income, and deriving strength from what we have really accomplished—regardless of what others may think and say.

If we are confident in our principles, standards, faith, and actions, we do not need to fear the rejection or ridicule of those who do not share them.

My son-in-law Gian faced such a challenge while attending law school in Massachusetts. In a class discussing censorship, the professor announced he was going to show a video clip of a comedy routine that had been deemed offensive by the Federal Communications Commission. In a condescending tone the professor announced, "It's no big deal. I don't think this is that bad at all. But I don't want to hear complaints later, so if you are going to be offended you can leave now."

Gian closed up his laptop and stood to leave. The professor rolled his eyes and exhaled loudly. Some of the students seated around Gian were shocked that someone actually stood up. Then another man stood and followed Gian. A few seconds later, yet another man left.

Once outside, one classmate said, "I'm glad we did that."

The other added, "Thanks for getting up, you guys. I was uncomfortable and didn't want to stay, but I didn't want to be the only one to leave."

Later that day, Gian was surprised when two women who were in the class approached him and said, "We wanted to leave too, but we were too embarrassed. We didn't want anyone to think we were prudes. You guys are true gentlemen." Gian acted with so much confidence that instead of laughing at him or ridiculing him, several students followed him, and others who didn't have his confidence admired his choice.

As shown by Gian's experience, we cannot realize how many people who are seeking light may be noticing our choices and our behavior. A young man said, "I've always been able to tell the difference between right and wrong, and I've known the ways I should behave. But I hadn't really had the courage to do this. Then I met some friends who actually lived by their principles and standards. They gave me the support I needed to do what I should and become the kind of person I wanted to be."

REPLACE FEAR WITH FAITH

"Wherefore take unto you the whole armour of God, that ye may be able . . . to stand" (Ephesians 6:13). Paul outlined the preparation for battle against our fears: the girdle was truth, the breastplate was righteousness, the shoes were "the gospel of peace," the shield was faith, the helmet was salvation, and the final weapon was "the sword of the Spirit, which is the word of God" (Ephesians 6:14–17). Faith is to fear what light is to darkness. They can't coexist. When light appears, darkness wanes. When one takes on the armor of God, fear retreats into the shadows.

We don't usually think of armor and Miss America in the same sentence, but former Miss America Sharlene Wells Hawkes described that the armor of God was exactly what she needed as she overcame fears:

"In the aftermath of the Miss America pageant . . . , I had an opportunity to frequently describe [my] standards. . . . It's a bit scary to literally stand before the world and answer any questions the media people dare ask. As I went into my first press conference, I wondered almost the same things I had wondered my first day of junior high or high school: *Will they approve of me, like me, accept me? Am I going to be sophisticated enough to satisfy their expectations? What kinds of questions will I be asked?*

> *When one takes on the armor of God, fear retreats into the shadows.*

"To be honest, when I first walked into the room and saw it full of media 'vultures' who looked as though they wanted to pick me apart, I began to doubt myself a little.

I wondered if it was going to be necessary to expose all the things that would make me appear strange, out of touch, and 'squeaky clean.' Part of me wanted to be accepted, to be seen as 'with it.' . . . But it only took a moment to put that temptation aside. I realized that what I was feeling was fear—fear of what they might say or write about me. Fear that I would be perceived as too different to represent the young women of America. Fear of their opinions. And I didn't even know them! I should have been far more concerned about the opinions of those I care about most: my family, my Heavenly Father, even myself" (*Living in but Not of the World,* 19–20).

Now Sharlene likes to remind people of a formula she has learned: "One + God = the Majority." We may never face crowds of reporters like Sharlene did, but the same formula can help us. As long as we are with God, we are in the majority. So some people are laughing and pointing fingers; so what? Being pointed at shouldn't bother anyone who is pointed in the right direction.

In Old Testament times, the crowds laughed and pointed at Noah, but in the end it wasn't Noah who missed the boat. In New Testament times, nonbelievers cast out Stephen and stoned him. Paul was ridiculed and reviled. People said he was completely crazy. "Be not afraid," the Lord told Paul, "for I am with thee" (Acts 18:9–10). Paul courageously declared, "I am not ashamed of the gospel of Christ," and, "If God be for us, who can be against us?" (Romans 1:16; 8:31).

I have met people today who show Paul-like faith and strength in living their standards, even when the likely disapproval might have negative effects. A man on the East Coast who badly needed a job was given an interview. His potential employer wasted no time in outlining his expectations, which included working on Sundays. The man said, "I would rather not work on Sunday. My family is religious."

The interviewer was shocked. He said, "Listen here, if I hire you, you will work on Sundays."

The man met the employer's gaze, leaned across the desk, and said, "Sir, if you hire me, I'll work so hard on the other days of the week that you won't even need me on Sunday." Not only did the man get the job on his stated terms, but the boss called his own supervisor and said, "Never in all my years have I seen someone show such backbone. This guy should run for president. We need people like that running the country."

Bees? Sharks? Thunder? Vacuums? What is your worst fear? Maybe some of your deepest fears are "people fears"— possibly facing rejection, humiliation, and embarrassment before others. When people put you down or push you to the limit, remember you are not the only one to face such persecution and negative pressure.

Jesus Christ had many self-appointed critics who followed Him throughout His life. He said to His followers, "Blessed are ye, when men shall revile you, and persecute you, and shall say all manner of evil against you falsely, for my sake. Rejoice, and be exceeding glad . . . for so persecuted they the prophets which were before you" (Matthew 5:11–12). Christ was betrayed and unjustly arrested. He was persecuted and mocked. Yet through it all He expected the best. When some did turn on Him, He understood all that was behind their hateful cries and gestures. Did He not say, "for they know not what they do" (Luke 23:34)?

When others mocked and belittled, Jesus didn't retract His teachings or undo His miracles. He didn't stop doing what He knew was right because of what others thought. The Savior showed no fear. Rather, He acted with pure and perfect confidence. No wonder our faith in Him can replace every fear.

CHAPTER SEVEN

SEVEN DAYS OF RE-CREATION

I once wrote a little poem called "New Year's Resolutions" in which I described the problem with depending entirely on willpower to make positive changes:

> *On January first with pen in hand*
> *I list my hopes and fears.*
> *I think I'd save myself some time*
> *If I just copied last year's.*

Choosing to be a 7-day Christian is choosing to be changed. Just as the earth went through 7 days of creation, we must also go through 7 days of re-creation. My friend Rich Tenney helped me see that the pattern God used when He created the earth is the same pattern He is using as He is re-creating us. The earth was formed, divided, enlightened, beautified, and filled with life as it was prepared to be inhabited by us. Then the Lord rested. Now we are going through the same process.

FORMED

In the book of Genesis we learn, "God created the heaven and the earth. And the earth was without form" (1:1–2). The Lord shaped, organized, and formed the earth. Later in the Old Testament we learn about how He can also shape, organize, and form us: "But now, O Lord, thou art our father; we are the clay, and thou our potter; and we all are the work of thy hand" (Isaiah 64:8). True change is a spiritual quest. The reshaping begins internally before it occurs externally, just as the design for a useful pot takes shape in the mind of a potter before it is molded with physical materials.

I have sometimes seen any attempts I was making at self-improvement as just that—attempts *I* was making. I had to realize that true change occurs only as God works in me and through me. If I amount to any good, it is only because He is good. Becoming a 7-day Christian means I relinquish any idea that I am in charge, in control, or capable of making positive changes by myself. I recognize my complete dependence on God and surrender myself like a lump of clay into His hands. If I once said, "I can do hard things," I replace it with "I can do all things through Christ which strengtheneth me" (Philippians 4:13).

For example, the day I turned fifty, I did something I

had not done for years: I weighed myself. I knew that I had put on a few extra pounds, but I had fooled myself into thinking it really wasn't all that much. The moment of truth made me realize I had a big problem—literally.

I knew I had to do something about it, but I had tried many diets before and usually ended up gaining back the weight I had lost and more. I had started exercise programs, but they never lasted. How could I change?

> *True change occurs only as God works in me and through me. If I amount to any good, it is only because He is good.*

At first I tried to pretend I didn't need to. I looked around at friends my age and saw that I was not the only one suffering from an expanded waistline. As much as I tried to rationalize that I was just getting more huggable, I still felt angry at myself for not showing a little self-discipline and restraint.

A few days later I drove to a mountain lodge where I had been invited to speak to a large youth gathering. There I ran into Cody Sanders—a young woman who had once been in my sixth-grade class. "Mr. Wilcox," she said, "do you remember me?" Of course I did. How could I forget this little fireball of a student who played "Ringa Turner" (imitating the then-popular singer Tina Turner) in that year's Christmas production?

"So tell me what you have been up to," I urged. Cody

filled me in on how she had married and had two children. I told her about what my wife and kids were doing. It was a happy reunion.

As we began to say good-bye, Cody said, "I remember you loved peanut M&Ms and pepperoni pizza, so I brought you a bag and a gift certificate, but I can't in good conscience give you junk food without also giving you a gift certificate for some fitness training." Turns out that Cody had become a personal trainer and owner of a fitness studio. She gave me the gifts and a hug, and I was on my way.

The whole way down the canyon I wanted to eat the M&Ms, but right next to them was the gift certificate for fitness training. It took all the fun out of it. I had heard of personal trainers before, but I believed they worked for rich people; they seemed like a luxury I could never afford. "Besides," I told myself, "you don't need anyone's help. You can do it alone." I got home and put Cody's card in my drawer.

Over the next few days I determined to try harder to eat right and exercise. When I got on the scale to see the results of all my hard work, I found I had actually gained. "What's the use?" I complained to my wife. "I can't do this. Why should I even try? Where's the ice cream?"

The following day I regretted my binge and felt worse than ever. I retrieved Cody's card and called her. I felt a little embarrassed that the teacher was asking his former student for help, but deep down I knew I couldn't do it alone. Cody answered the phone, and we set an appointment. "I'm afraid I can't afford to do this," I confessed.

She said, "Mr. Wilcox, you can't afford *not* to do this. Think of the difference this will make in your life." She was right, and she even offered me the "former teacher discount." I considered how many piano lessons my wife and I had paid for through the years for the kids, as well as all the sports camps and dance lessons. If I had found a way to provide braces for my kids' teeth, surely I could find a way to invest a little in my own well-being.

The time of the first session arrived. "Cody," I spoke solemnly. "Promise me two things: (1) don't you dare let me quit, and (2) don't make me run." I had bad memories of running laps in PE classes when I was younger, particularly of how humiliating it was to get so far behind the other students that I would look like I was leading the pack. Cody promised, and we began. In private, I reached out to God in prayer and asked for His help and blessings.

It is said that when people get trapped in quicksand, the worst thing they can do is try to get out on their own. The more they struggle, the more quickly they sink. Only as they stretch out their arms and legs as far as they can are they able to slow their descent and call for others to help them. When we get ourselves caught in negative cycles of compulsive or discouraging behavior, our hope for rescue is to reach out and allow God and others to help us. This is how we can be formed and reformed.

DIVIDED

In the creation narrative Moses wrote: "God . . . divided the waters which were under the firmament from the waters which were above the firmament. . . . And God said, Let the waters under the heaven be gathered together unto one place, and let the dry land appear: and it was so. (Genesis 1:7–9).

As we strive to become 7-day Christians, God will help us to make necessary divisions in our lives. He will help us separate what matters from what doesn't.

In my fitness journey, God helped me progress by dividing my past from my future—years of failed attempts from the possibility of success. He helped me to divide truth from rationalizations and excuses. As the "water" was pushed aside, the "dry land" began to appear, and suddenly I had a firm foundation on which to build.

Previously in my life, every diet or exercise program had been an event—a period through which I would grit my teeth and endure until I could get back to normal life. This attitude provided a watery foundation, and I slipped and slid all over the place. This time, God helped me find dry land. My work with Cody was not a program or event, but a lifestyle change. I was in this for the long haul. I was not starting a program with a beginning, precise guidelines, and an end; I was committing to a change that—through all the ups and downs—was not going to be abandoned or forgotten. This long-term perspective was firm ground.

In the past, when I would mess up, I would give up. I would think, *I've blown it now. I might as well not even try anymore.* This all-or-nothing mentality was evidence that I had been thinking only short-term. I had been looking at daily successes or failures and nothing beyond that. I determined to expand my thinking. If being fit is just something a doctor suggests, I can blow it off. If I see it as part of who I am and who I want to be, that's different. A temporary diet I can quit; a new way of life is different—as different as land and water.

The first promise Cody made to me, she kept. The second, she didn't.

Several months into my training, Cody said, "Remember how you said you didn't want to run? Well, we're just going to have you run on the treadmill for half a minute." I figured I could do anything for half a minute. Over the next few weeks, a half minute turned into one, then two, then five minutes. Soon Cody announced that she had signed me up to run my first 5K on Thanksgiving Day. She didn't understand. I didn't run on Thanksgiving Day—I ate! "Not this year," she said. "In sixth grade you used to tell us about getting out of our comfort zones. Well, it's that time!" Caught by my own advice! As much as I didn't want to admit it, I knew Cody was right. It was time to trust God and those He had placed in my path.

As the Thanksgiving Day run approached, Cody helped me prepare. She assisted me in altering my eating habits— bad habits I had struggled with my whole life. She helped me train and build stamina for the run. A 5K is nothing for most people, but the thought of it was overwhelming to me. Some days were better than others. Progress was slow—definitely two steps forward and one step back. Still, I hung in there. Nothing was as helpful as having to be accountable to someone who really cared about me and wanted the best for me. Another helpful activity was memorizing scriptures. I would recite them to myself when I ran because it distracted me.

My fitness journey demonstrates but does not comprise all our experiences with important divisions in our lives. All that is good, we recognize because of contrast. We know health as it is divided from sickness. We know pleasure as it is divided from pain. We rejoice in freedom when we contrast it with bondage. We feel the unspeakable joy of our Savior's love as we contrast it with the despair we might have felt when we thought that we were facing our trials alone. These divisions help us as we are being re-created.

ENLIGHTENED

"And God made two great lights: the greater light to rule the day, and the lesser light to rule the night: he made the stars also . . . to give light upon the earth" (Genesis 1:16–17). From the beginning, the world has never been left in complete darkness. Even at night, light rules.

As dark as it sometimes seems and as discouraged as we

sometimes become, light rules. Recall the Savior's words as recorded in John 8:12, "I am the light of the world: he that followeth me shall not walk in darkness, but shall have the light of life." We all face difficult temptations, and we may feel we are walking in darkness. But we must recognize that the only power Satan has is what we choose to give him. God, who is the source of power and light, loves us; Satan is not capable of love.

Our journey to become 7-day Christians is never easy. We climb to mountain peaks of success and lose our way in valleys of failure. God is willing to help us during both the highs and lows. God did not remove the Red Sea, He opened it; He will help us find a way through our problems as well. The light does not always reveal distant landscapes; sometimes it gives us just enough vision to get us through one day at a time.

> *God did not remove the Red Sea, He opened it; He will help us find a way through our problems as well.*

John Henry Newman, one of the most acclaimed English philosophers and clergymen of the nineteenth century, wrote the poem "The Pillar of the Cloud" during a time of intense frustration when circumstances were preventing him from doing work he perceived as a sacred calling. It is widely loved and sung today as the hymn "Lead, Kindly Light":

Lead, kindly Light, amid th'encircling gloom;
Lead thou me on!
The night is dark, and I am far from home;
Lead thou me on!
Keep thou my feet; I do not ask to see
The distant scene—one step enough for me.

The journey to becoming a 7-day Christian takes time. We must be patient with ourselves because we never arrive quickly at any destination worth reaching. Strength too easily won is not really strength at all. When we are tempted to lose patience, we must look for God's light. There may not be enough to see "the distant scene," but there is always enough light for us to take "one step."

One big step for me on my fitness journey was that first 5K. Thanksgiving Day arrived, and I met Cody and her husband, Trevor, at the location of the race. Some of my family came to run along with me. On the outside I tried to keep a positive attitude, but inside I felt nervous. All the fears and inadequacies I had ever had about my lack of athletic abilities surfaced. I had to keep pushing them away. I had never done something like this before. I was definitely stretching out of my comfort zone. My goal was to finish the full race without stopping—something I had yet to accomplish in all my training. Could I really do it?

I lined up with the hundreds of other runners, and suddenly we were off. Within the first few minutes many runners passed me—and that was after I had already placed myself toward the back of the group. Still I plodded forward. In my mind I started reciting my scriptures, beginning with Genesis 1:1–3: "In the beginning God created the heaven and the earth. And the earth was without form, and void; and darkness was upon the face of the deep. And the Spirit of God moved upon the face of the waters. And God said, Let there be light: and there was light."

I appreciated my kids staying by me. Of course, they were walking as fast as I was running, but they kept telling me I was doing a good job, so I didn't give up. When I finally crossed the finish line—after running the whole way—I thought it was appropriate that I was reciting the Twenty-Third Psalm: "Yea, though I walk through the valley of the shadow of death . . ." I felt dead, but I had finished.

In life, as in 5Ks, I have learned that we do not need to be in competition with others for speed or skills—only with ourselves. "It doesn't matter how we place, but it is absolutely critical that we finish" (Mike McKinley, *Am I Really a Christian?* 14).

In the weeks and months that followed that first 5K, I realized that the creation scripture I had been reciting, "Let there be light," was actually shedding light on my whole ordeal. What started as a strategy for keeping my mind distracted actually began helping me make sense of all I was experiencing. God's light is vital as we are re-created.

BEAUTIFIED

"And the earth brought forth grass, and herb yielding seed after his kind, and the tree yielding fruit, whose seed was in itself, after his kind" (Genesis 1:12). God beautified the earth with an amazing variety of trees and other plants, which all bring forth seeds and fruits. In Ecclesiastes 3:11 we read that God "hath made every thing beautiful in his time."

We live in a society in which beauty is defined in artificial and negative ways. Individuals damage their health—physical, mental, and spiritual—with eating disorders. Cosmetics and fashions are powerful trendsetters as well as profitable businesses. The Savior defined beauty differently:

"Consider the lilies of the field, how they grow; they toil not, neither do they spin: And yet I say unto you, that even Solomon in all his glory was not arrayed like one of these. Wherefore, if God so clothe the grass of the field, which to day is and to morrow is cast into the oven, shall he not much more clothe you" (Matthew 6:28–30).

The beauty in the re-creation of self comes from the deep love and concern for others that are a part of our love for and emulation of our Savior. This beauty can be as natural in us as in the lilies God created for our joy and instruction.

As with the lesson in the lilies, Jesus often used his creations, including beautiful and useful plant life, in teaching important truths. For example, "Ye shall know them by their fruits. Do men gather grapes of thorns, or figs of thistles?" (Matthew 7:16). The Savior used fruit to represent all that is good and nourishing. We know we are progressing as we should when we see our lives filled with beautiful fruits—experiences, service, healthy perceptions—that are pure and sweet.

Reflecting on my fitness journey, I know people who have learned to love eating healthy foods and exercising regularly. I am not quite there yet, but I am heading in the right direction. As I keep try-ing, I see precious fruits mani-fest in my own life. I find I am happier because I am showing some self-discipline. I am more confident when I interact with others. I find myself being less self-conscious and better able to focus outward. I also find I have more energy to keep up with the demands of life. These fruits are making my life sweeter.

> *We know we are progressing as we should when we see our lives filled with beautiful fruits— experiences, service, healthy perceptions—that are pure and sweet.*

In Psalm 149:4 we are assured that "the Lord . . . will beautify the meek with salvation." What greater beauty could we ask of God? Just as God beautified the earth, He beautifies us as we are re-created.

FILLED

"And God said, Let the waters bring forth abundantly the moving creature that hath life, and fowl that may fly above the earth. . . . Let the earth bring forth the living creature after his kind, cattle, and creeping thing, and beast of the earth after his kind" (Genesis 1:20–24).

With beautiful and useful plants in abundance, the world was ready to be filled with animal life. It is now full of so much to appreciate, love, and savor, but sometimes we miss those joys completely. Even though the earth is full, we can still feel empty. Becoming 7-day Christians means learning to love what God loves.

Think of something you have learned to love—something that now fills you with joy—that you didn't initially like. You may be thinking about listening to an opera, attending church, or eating tomatoes. Whatever the activity, changing your attitude was not a matter of just doing something until you got used to it. The change had more to do with seeing beyond the activity itself to something greater. Perhaps opera touched your emotions. Attending church meetings helped you lift those around you and feel closer to God. Eating tomatoes made you feel healthier. These activities might have started as items to be checked off a list, but as your perspective broadened, your motives matured, and these activities became a regular part of your life. Now you probably can't imagine not engaging in them, and you may even feel genuine sadness for those who are not able to experience the joy that you feel. Your listening, attending, and even eating stopped being ends in themselves and became instead means to greater ends—emotional, spiritual, and physical growth. This fulfillment is the power of broader vision—seeing "afar off" (Genesis 22:4; Hebrews 11:13).

With this enlarged vision, we can see and appreciate not only the fullness in the world around us but the fullness of our own lives as well. We can be filled with a renewed sense of purpose and joy. We can see the world as God sees it—and we can see ourselves as God sees us. Being filled with this perspective is essential as we are re-created.

"IN THE IMAGE OF GOD"

Think of the sacred words of the psalmist:

"When I consider thy heavens, the work of thy fingers, the moon and the stars, which thou hast ordained;

"What is man, that thou art mindful of him? And the son of man, that thou visitest him?

"For thou hast made him a little lower than the angels, and hast crowned him with glory and honour.

"Thou madest him to have dominion over the works of thy hands; thou hast put all things under his feet" (Psalm 8:3–8).

From this psalm we recognize that even the earth was not created as an end in itself, but as a means to a greater end. During the creation, "God saw every thing that he had made, and, behold, it was very good" (Genesis 1:31). But good for what? It had to be good for something greater: "So God created man in his own image, in the image of God created he him; male and female created he them" (Genesis 1:27). The earth's formation, division, enlightenment, beautification (with plants), and fulfillment (with animals) was for a greater purpose than merely existing. God made it for us.

Like the earth, 7-day Christians are being re-created for a greater purpose than just taking up space. We must allow a greater purpose to inform our actions. Considering my fitness journey, always in the past my efforts at weight loss and exercise were ends in themselves—mostly so I could fit in my clothes and look better. That self-centered purpose wasn't too satisfying or motivating. It was too easy to stop caring about what I looked like and give all my "skinny" clothes to Goodwill. This time I tried to find a greater purpose.

I determined I wanted to try to be a better example to others. I wanted to be fit in order to better serve others, provide for my family, and do God's work. This time I told myself I was making changes in my life not just so I could look good or even feel good, but because I wanted to *do* good and *be* good. I may not yet love eating vegetables as much as pizza and candy, but I love God and desire to serve Him enough to pass on the pizza and candy a little more often than I used to. I may not love exercising, but I love my family and want to be around as long as I can to keep assisting them. Love for God and others gives me the motivation to keep trying.

However long it takes, we proceed one consistent step at a time. That concept has become a personal theme for me—especially since my life started including running.

Two and a half years after I began working with Cody, I ran my first half marathon. To help me prepare, my daughter Whitney would run with me. Night after night, mile after mile, one consistent step at a time, we ran. One evening we went on our run and, as usual, I fell behind my daughter. On our way home, I was about twenty feet behind Whitney when my son-in-law, Gian, drove past us in his car and panicked. He saw Whitney running home and some old man chasing her in the dark! He almost stopped the car to rush to her defense when he suddenly realized the old man was his father-in-law.

On the night before the half marathon, three of my kids—Russell, Trish, and Whitney—who were going to run it with me gave me a sign to wear: "If found on ground, please drag across finish line." The next morning we got up at 3:00 a.m., boarded our bus about 4:00, and started the race at 6:00 a.m. with three thousand other runners. For many it was obviously just one more run in a lifetime full of them. For me it was a turning point, a milestone, a first. I had lost fifty pounds and was at the lowest weight I had been for over ten years. (I actually lost much more than fifty pounds because I kept having to lose the same pounds over and over again.) Believe it or not, I finished the half marathon. I ran 13.1 miles without stopping!

Along with feeling the support of Cody and my family, I was buoyed up by many friends I made along the way. There was the encouraging fireman who ran at about my same pace to keep me going, even though he could have run much faster. There was the tall runner who patted my shoulders and shouted positive words when I was at the halfway point. There were strangers who honked and cheered from their cars as they passed all the runners on the other side of the road.

The greatest temptation to give up came when I was running a distance I had never run before. The most I had run at one time was eleven miles, so miles twelve and thirteen were killers for me. Music helped. I loved listening to upbeat songs through my earphones. The music moved me forward.

Nothing felt better than seeing my family at the finish line. All I wanted was to hold my wife, Debi, and all my kids in my arms. There is a powerful bond felt by those engaged in doing difficult and important things together. I will never forget gathering Russell, Trish, and Whitney into a sweaty group hug. We were a good team.

That day I went home and enjoyed a hot shower and a long nap. "And on the seventh day God ended his work which he had made; and he rested . . . from all his work which he had made" (Genesis 2:2). I'm grateful God lets me rest now and then too.

That half marathon will not be the last time I run. I know there will be more races in my future because exercise is not an event. It is now part of my way of life, and God knows I am not doing it just for me.

Formed, divided, enlightened, beautified, and filled with life—the phases of the creation can teach us about phases through which God takes each of us as we become 7-day Christians. We are being re-created for Him and by Him, and it is "very good" (Genesis 1:31).

CHAPTER EIGHT

RIGHT LANE MUST TURN RIGHT

Because I travel so much, I see a lot of funny signs. I once saw a store with a large sign announcing "Store closing," but posted just above the front doors was another sign that said, "Now hiring." At one intersection, a stop sign was on the same post as another sign that read, "No stopping any time." In a park there was a "No pets allowed" sign next to another that said, "All pets must be on leash." I also liked this one: "Caution. Water on road during rain." And then there was the "Lodging next right" sign posted just above "State Prison." Perhaps my favorite sign is on a hospital in Japan near where my son used to live. It wouldn't have been funny to the Japanese, but it gave English speakers a good laugh. The name of the hospital was two Japanese characters: *Ai dai* (pronounced "I die"). I don't think I want to be admitted to that hospital.

Once while I was driving I saw a sign that read, "Right

lane must turn right." At first that seemed like a no-brainer, but the more I thought about it, the more the sign took on a personal meaning. As a follower of Christ, my direction is clear. When I am in the right lane, I must turn right. There really is no other choice, no going back.

OBEDIENCE AND SACRIFICE

Tito Momen was a Muslim who converted to Christianity. He was born in Nigeria and raised to be a leader among clerics. When he encountered Christianity and became a believer, his fiancée rejected him. His father disowned him. His family held a public funeral for him, and his mother, who felt responsible for his conversion, committed suicide. Later, on trumped-up charges, he was imprisoned in Egypt, where he faced horrific abuse because of his faith. For fifteen years he languished in the most dismal circumstances imaginable. Not only was he persecuted mercilessly, but his health failed him. There were moments of despair in which he would think that if he had never become Christian, his life would have been so different. He knew if he were willing to forsake his faith, his circumstances would be better. Still, something deep inside him assured him he had made the right choice. Denying it would be turning his back on the only thing that really mattered. Many small miracles finally led to his release and receipt of clemency in Ghana (see Tito Momen and Jeff Benedict, *My Name Used to Be Muhammad*).

Tito's faith is like that of Peter and the other Apostles, who were asked by the Savior, "Will ye also go away?" (John 6:67).

"Then Simon Peter answered him, Lord, to whom shall we go? thou hast the words of eternal life. And we believe and are sure that thou art that Christ, the Son of the living God" (John 6:68–69). Peter and the Apostles were in the right lane. There was no other option but to follow wherever it led. Tito Momen had made the same commitment.

Mike McKinley wrote that in the past "true Christians endured persecution for the sake of Christ. They were publicly humiliated and financially ruined, but they clung tightly to Jesus and did not turn back. Like all believers throughout time, they had experienced the new birth and pledged their fealty to Jesus. No amount of trouble could pry them loose. Conversely, those who profess faith in Christ but then abandon him when trials hit were probably never genuinely Christians in the first place" (*Am I Really a Christian?* 83–84).

Unfortunately, not everybody who is in the right lane is willing to turn right. Turning left from a right lane of traffic may or may not have serious and dangerous consequences; turning away from Christ always does. In Luke 17:32 the Savior counseled, "Remember Lot's wife." Lot's wife may not seem like a major scripture character to many Christians, but the Savior himself called attention to what happened to her. Lot and his family were warned to escape from Sodom and Gomorrah before the destruction of these cities, with the condition, "Look not behind thee . . . ; escape to the mountain, lest thou be consumed" (Genesis 19:17). Lot's wife apparently missed the offerings of Sodom and Gomorrah. Perhaps she was angry that the Lord expected her to leave. She looked back. She chose to be a pillar of salt rather than the salt of the earth (see Matthew 5:13).

> *Many people in the world believe in God; some even express great love and gratitude for Him. But few are willing to put their time, talents, and treasure where their mouths are.*

True faith leads to obedience and sacrifice. Many people in the world believe in God; some even express great love and gratitude for Him. But few are willing to put their time, talents, and treasure where their mouths are. Life in the right lane requires right turns. Unlike Lot's wife, we must look to the future with courage and hope.

GOSPEL COMMITMENTS

My friend Sheri Dew, who was once invited to be a White House delegate and private sector adviser to the Commission on the Status of Women, recalled her first initiation into the right lane at the age of eight, as her grandmother told her that "Jesus Christ is our Savior" and that when you know this "your life can never be the same again" (*No Doubt about It,* 26). In considering a statement like that, we might quickly ask if a prosperous grandmother was describing her easy life to an idealistic child. Actually, Sheri Dew's grandmother survived both the Dust Bowl and the Depression homesteading a farm in Kansas: "Some days the dust was so heavy that if farmer or livestock were caught in the fields, they suffocated for lack of oxygen" (*No Doubt about It,* 56). Their farm did not come through unscathed—but their faith did.

Two generations later, Sheri reflected: "I am grateful that during the intervening years I have come to know for myself that Jesus is the Christ, our Savior and our Redeemer, and that once you have that knowledge your life can never be the same" (*No Doubt about It,* 26).

Christian conviction, conversion, and commitment brought a grandmother through physical and emotional devastations from both natural and economic disasters and also helped a granddaughter navigate all the difficulties that have come her way.

A friend who is currently serving a sentence in a maximum security U.S. prison has learned much about living gospel commitments even in the most trying conditions. He wrote me the following in a letter: "I made mistakes to end up where I am, but instead of turning from God I am trying to return to Him and live His gospel. It's especially difficult in this environment, but lately I've been contemplating the incredibly personal nature of our relationship with God. Faith is required at every level. Not simply a faith that He can bless us and save us, but faith that He knows the best way to bless us and save us. When times get hard and I become discouraged, I pray for the faith of Polycarp and I continue forward."

Polycarp was a second-century bishop in Smyrna, an ancient Greek city located within the borders of present-day Turkey. He lived in a time of great persecution from the Romans. When a sentence of death was passed on Polycarp because of his faith, the Roman official gave him a chance not just to live but to go free if he denied his faith in Christ. Polycarp explained he had served Christ for more than eighty years, and Christ had never done him any wrong. He boldly responded that he could not blaspheme the King who had saved him.

The Roman magistrate assured Polycarp he would be consumed in a fiery death, but Polycarp was fearless and undaunted. According to tradition, the flames miraculously failed to harm him, and so a Roman soldier stabbed him to death.

My friend in prison wrote:

"As I read about noble Polycarp I suddenly imagined his thoughts during those final traumatic moments. Certainly he knew the history of God's dealings with His people in earlier ages. I wonder if he found courage and strength in the example of Shadrach, Meshach, and Abednego recorded in Daniel 3, who suffered through a similar circumstance. I wonder if Polycarp expected to be saved and delivered like those who exercised faith before him. Was he confident that a miracle would also spare him? As the soldiers tied him up and lit the fire, was Polycarp looking around for his own angel? Was he expecting his own deliverance? As the flames grew larger and Polycarp was untouched, was he surprised? Then when the Roman lunged toward him and stabbed him, did he wonder why God saved others, but not him? Such analogous experiences, yet with such different conclusions. Shadrach and the others left the flames unharmed. Polycarp's miracle started the same, but instead ended in death. These were two different conclusions to the same demonstration of faith. I guess the point is that they all showed the same faith. They trusted God whether or not things turned out as they hoped. They trusted not just His ability to save them, but His methods."

My friend's words touched me deeply—especially considering his own difficult circumstances. He concluded his letter by saying: "Brad, I don't pretend to know much. My faith is so simple. But I trust God. I want to walk in His way and keep my commitments to Him. I see His love and kindness everywhere I look—even in this place that most would describe as 'God forsaken.'"

HIGHER GROUND

My friend in prison was learning, as did Sheri Dew and her grandmother, that the farther we progress along the path of Christian discipleship, the steeper it becomes. But when we are committed to the right lane, then even when the right lane goes uphill and becomes more challenging,

> *The farther we progress along the path of Christian discipleship, the steeper it becomes.*

we can't make a U-turn to look for an easier road. Such roads exist, but they do not lead where we need to go.

Some are confused when they try to draw closer to God and find themselves facing greater problems and temptations than they did previously. Suddenly they are more aware of their weaknesses than ever before. They wonder how they can feel farther from God when they were trying to be closer to Him. To one degree or another, all 7-day Christians have experienced this phenomenon. An author I admire, Neal A. Maxwell, wrote, "If we are serious about our discipleship, Jesus will eventually request each of us to do those very things which are the most difficult for us to do" (*A Time to Choose,* 46). Thus, "sometimes the best people . . . have the worst experiences . . . because they are the most ready to learn" (*Disciple's Life,* 20).

Powerful words! The author went far beyond writing them. He lived them as he fought valiantly against leukemia. Many who are diagnosed with a terminal illness become angry with God. They lift a clenched fist toward heaven and declare that God has abandoned them. This man chose to lift an open, submissive hand, seeking God's help. He saw himself as passing through a time of divine tutoring and refining. He said, "Adversity can squeeze out of us the [remaining] hypocrisy that's there. [So, for me,] it's been a great spiritual adventure, one I would not want to have missed. . . . And even though this has [had high costs], it's been a great blessing" (*Disciple's Life*, 558–59).

In Luke 12:48 we read, "For unto whomsoever much is given, of him shall be much required: and to whom men have committed much, of him they will ask the more." When we choose the right lane, we are given much, but much is also required. Those who choose Christ find that His refining, sanctifying process is rarely quick or easy.

My friend Robert L. Millet wrote: "Perplexing and ponderous and painful as it may seem, you and I have been commissioned to stand on higher ground, to turn the other cheek, to forgive and to desire the best for those who hurt us, and even to pray for them. Further, as the Master said, we are to love them! Boy, this Christianity business is tough" (in *A Year of Powerful Prayer*, 382).

It's one thing to steer your vehicle to the right. But rocks and ruts in the road can make the ride uncomfortable. Matters of forgiving, desiring the best, and praying for those who hurt us can be among the most difficult of our Christian commitments. Even a commandment as seemingly straightforward and simple as honoring parents (see Exodus 20:12) can require much.

One girl wrote, "My father doesn't live with us anymore, but you have no idea how much what he did and does affects me. It is as if he is still there and I can't escape his negative influences."

A man wrote, "My dad left my mother and chose to live

a lifestyle that has brought nothing but pain and sorrow to him and to our family. I fake like it doesn't bother me, but deep down it eats at me every day."

Another man wrote, "My mother always abused us, not physically but mentally and emotionally. She manipulated my sisters and me and made us feel totally worthless."

How do these people honor such dishonorable parents? The answer to such a question is personal; we need to step far outside our comfort zones. It may take many years to resolve such deep hurt, anger, and frustration. Nevertheless, those in the right lane must turn right. Christ's lane gives us obligations, opportunities, and blessings simultaneously.

A woman I will call Sue was sexually abused from her early childhood. Her father threatened that if she told what he was doing or refused to comply with his demands, he would turn the abuse on her youngest sister. Her mother knew what was going on but did nothing. Finally, the father divorced the family to marry his secretary, making legal provisions to prevent his former wife and children from receiving financial support of any kind. Although the father was wealthy, the family suffered deprivation and misery.

Years later, when Sue was a young adult living in a different state, her father killed himself. At his funeral, his secretary-wife mockingly told Sue that her father had done worse things than Sue realized, which included raping the little sister Sue had suffered to protect. When Sue returned from the funeral, her friends used the phrase "in darkness" to describe her. To her, her father was beyond anyone's forgiveness; even his self-brutal death did not seem punishment enough. She wanted to despise him, yet he was her father, and Sue had committed to Christian living. All she could see was darkness threatening to engulf her.

Later, Sue had a deeply religious experience in which she learned that she did not need to try to judge her father. God's ways and His judgments are not necessarily our ways and our judgments, she was told. God's knowledge of her life and her father's life was perfect; she needed to trust God. Relieved of the need to sort out judgment, Sue felt the darkness lift as she put judgment in the hands of the Lord and felt His healing influence.

Perhaps we may not face trials as severe as those faced by Sue, but in one way or another we all have to deal with the consequences of the poor choices made by others. Sometimes the effects of such choices are only inconvenient and bothersome, but sometimes they can be devastating and life altering. We may feel totally justified to give in to hate, to strike back, to lash out in revenge, and to hurt as we have been hurt. We can withhold forgiveness, clinging to the false belief that by doing so we are somehow hurting someone besides ourselves. Despite the unfairness, pain, and abuse we have suffered, our choice to follow Christ in the right lane requires that we turn right toward higher ground.

Our damages, our needs, and ultimately our ways of coping will be ours individually, but our support, our comfort, and our guide can be Jesus Christ, who gives us the strength to persevere and the enabling power to do all that

He requires. Paul taught, "Work out your own salvation with fear and trembling. [But remember] it is God which worketh in you" (Philippians 2:12–13).

WITHHOLDING NOTHING

Mike McKinley wrote, "Here are the plain terms of discipleship. To be a Christian, you must literally be willing to die. You must count Jesus as more important than your own parents, siblings, and children" (*Am I Really a Christian?* 115; see also Luke 14:25–27).

When Cain's selfish sacrifice was not accepted by the Lord, "Cain was very wroth, and his countenance fell" (Genesis 4:5). Unlike Cain, Abel had chosen to withhold nothing from the Lord. In his anger and envy, "Cain rose up against Abel his brother, and slew him. And the Lord said unto Cain, Where is Abel thy brother? And he said, I know not: Am I my brother's keeper?" (Genesis 4:8–9).

Cain already knew the answer to this question. And he knew he had failed in the worst way possible to live that answer. To attempt to ease the personal hell he had created for himself, he tried to change the answer. In his prideful and unrepentant state, he tried to believe he was somehow justified. Many who behave like Cain attempt to cover the clock, but they can't change the time—for themselves or for others.

Although they were not responsible for their son's behavior, Adam and Eve had to deal with the loss and heartbreak caused by Cain's sin and try to protect the remainder of their family. Like those who must deal with parent or caretaker abuse, those who suffer from the serious misbehavior of sons, daughters, siblings, or peers have agony to deal with and challenges in going on with their lives. When staying in the right lane and turning right seems completely impossible, we can be comforted as we remember that "with God nothing shall be impossible" (Luke 1:37). We can proceed where He leads, withholding nothing.

Most of us don't start at this point of complete consecration. We begin by showing a willingness to obey and sacrifice. The closeness we feel to God due to our choices strengthens our faith and deepens our gospel commitments. This naturally moves us to live on higher ground. No longer do we obey and sacrifice out of desire for a reward or a feeling of duty or obligation. Finally we make our choices out of love. We withhold nothing from God because we love Him and His work so completely.

We all face circumstances in which the right-hand lane is inconvenient and even hazardous. We must be willing to obey and sacrifice for our faith in Jesus Christ, though for most of us prison will not be among our sacrifices, as it was for Tito Momen. We may never have to face death for

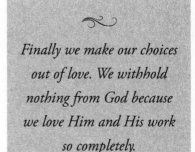

Finally we make our choices out of love. We withhold nothing from God because we love Him and His work so completely.

our gospel commitments, as did Polycarp, but we must realize that knowing Christ means our lives are never the same again. We will live commandments others don't live and have to accept suffering due to the actions of others. Through it all, we must be willing to forgive. It is part of living on higher ground and withholding nothing. We make these choices because we love God and He loves us. Filled with this love, we do not take any of these steps alone.

Christ said, "Come unto me, all ye that labour and are heavy laden, and I will give you rest. Take my yoke upon you, and learn of me. . . . For my yoke is easy, and my burden is light" (Matthew 11:28–30). Those who accept Christ's invitation will quickly learn that being a 7-day Christian is not a chore, but a joy. It is not restriction, but independence. It is not depletion, but complete and total fulfillment.

CHAPTER NINE

STANDING TOGETHER

In 1987 the United States celebrated the bicentennial of the signing of its Constitution, and I was teaching sixth grade. I wanted to help my class value the significance of the moment and sense the importance of this world-changing document. We memorized the Preamble. We reenacted the signing—complete with feathered pens and powdered wigs. I showed the children a picture of the chair used by George Washington during the Constitutional Convention, a chair with a carving of a half sun on it. I explained how Benjamin Franklin, the oldest signer, expressed his confidence in the nation's future by pointing at the carving and declaring the sun to be rising, not setting.

Despite all my efforts, some of the children still complained, "What does this have to do with us?"

I explained, "This document set forth our fundamental laws. It established our form of government and defined our rights and liberties." They still stared at me blankly. I guess those eleven-year-olds were too young to care about anything except how many minutes remained until their next recess.

Now my former students are grown, many of them with children of their own. I doubt they remember the facts we learned about the Constitution. However, their question—"What does this have to do with us?"—has remained with me. I would answer it differently today. I would say that in addition to all the information I taught them in 1987, the Constitution is also a monument to three personal qualities that we must all incorporate into our lives if we want our sun to be rising and not setting: collegiality, civility, and humility.

COLLEGIALITY

Collegiality is working effectively with others as colleagues despite differences. Historian Richard Beeman has explained that the representatives who attended the Constitutional Convention argued and debated passionately. Tempers flared during the day, but then these men put their strong opinions aside and dined together in the evenings as friends (see *Plain, Honest Men*). Are we willing to do the same with coworkers and neighbors who do not share all our views, values, and opinions—especially when it comes to religion? Can we set aside our personal and doctrinal differences long enough to work together as colleagues in a good cause?

A twenty-first-century woman named Margaret was not as fortunate as the Founding Fathers. When she attended her first convention in an unfamiliar city, she was a stranger except among a small number of individuals from her place of employment. After a busy day, the group from her home area

> *Can we set aside our personal and doctrinal differences long enough to work together as colleagues in a good cause?*

went to dinner together. One of the other women, Gwen, who had visited this city several times, insisted on a restaurant that she liked. The restaurant had a narrow specialty menu, consisting of foods that Margaret, a recent immigrant to the United States, disliked and felt she could not eat.

When Margaret explained her difficulty with this food, Gwen mocked her for behaving like a "spoiled child," shepherded the group into a taxi, and gave the address of the restaurant. Margaret declined to order food she knew she could not eat, so Gwen mocked her again and ordered a meal for her. Others in the group protested, but Gwen's scornful comments were continual and loud. Margaret did not eat the food, which would have made her ill, and Gwen scolded her throughout the meal, all the way back to the hotel, and repeatedly until the group had returned home. This violation of collegiality made all the participants tense and uncomfortable.

As part of my university work, I attend my share of

conferences and conventions and give my share of presentations for several national and international associations to which I belong. My work with the Association of Literacy Educators and Researchers (ALER) is the most fulfilling because of the collegiality that exists in that group. In other organizations I see a lot of competition between people pursuing their own self-serving agendas. I have seen audience members degrade other people's work and sharply criticize their research methods right in the middle of their presentations. In such moments I feel discouraged that professionals show so little professionalism.

At the ALER conferences, the atmosphere is different. People are respectful during the presentations but also during conversations in the hallways and at lunches and dinners. Like the representatives in the Constitutional Convention, ALER participants do not always agree on how to best handle the challenges in our professional field. We represent a wide variety of places, universities, religious backgrounds, and political leanings. Nevertheless, we are able to put differences aside and work together as colleagues. No one is forced to swallow either food or theories they find objectionable.

Collegiality is not just the stuff of constitutional conventions and professional organizations. It is a quality that is needed everywhere. I know three teens who have been successful in uniting people in collegiality for service from different age groups representing many different religions and denominations.

It all began with six-year-old Sam Barlow and his dad, Dave, playing a little game in which they expressed their love for each other. Sam would say, "I love you." Dave responded, "I love you more." Sam added, "I love you most." Then Dave always thought he had the ultimate word when he would say, "I love you infinity."

Once as they were going through their "who-loves-who-more war," Sam decided he was not going to be topped. When his dad said, "I love you infinity," Sam quickly replied, "I love you infinity and beyond!" Then his quick-thinking father said, "I love you infinity and beyond plus tax!" This declaration left both of them laughing and Sam searching for something greater than taxes.

The following day Sam rushed home from school and waited impatiently on the curb for his dad to come home from work. When Dave steered into the driveway and got out of the car, Sam rushed him and jumped into his arms. The boy hugged his father so fiercely that his body trembled as he whispered, "Python squeeze!" Then Sam leaned back, looked his father in the eyes, and said triumphantly, "Dad, I love you 206!" Dave was stumped. He didn't understand what his son was thinking. Sam saw his father's inquisitive look and said victoriously, "Today in school I learned that's how many bones there are in my body, so I love you 206! Dad, *that's every bone in my body!*"

That delightful interchange was the beginning of a service squad Sam and his brothers Corbin and Cayden launched several years later. They called it Team 206 (see www.servesquad.com or www.love206.com). Those who join with them commit to perform 206 hours of service or donate $206 to a worthy cause. Sam and his brothers chose Shriners Hospitals for Children. They earned $206 and donated it to support the creation of the Forever Young Zone at their local Shriners Hospital. The zone will provide a place in the hospital where children who lose an arm or leg can recover, socialize, and practice life skills using their prosthetic limbs or wheelchairs. NFL legend Steve Young had donated the bulk of the funds, but more was needed, and the Barlow boys stepped forward.

Others heard of Sam's donation and wanted to help too—including Miss America 2013, Mallory Hagan, and her chaperone, Marci Bowen. Marci told members of her Christian congregation in Arizona about Team 206, and several volunteered to help. Marci also told a friend in Hawaii who was from a different Christian denomination, and that friend joined with Sam, Corbin, and Cayden to help children in need. Team 206 now includes people from many religions and organizations who are putting differences aside and uniting in a spirit of true collegiality.

Another of the Barlow boys' ideas is to encourage everyone to set an alarm to go off at 2:06 each afternoon as a reminder to acknowledge someone in his or her life. I was the lucky recipient of one of those acknowledgments. It came from the boys' dad, Dave, who left the following phone message: "Brad, my alarm went off at 2:06 reminding me to acknowledge someone who has made a difference in my life, and today that someone is you." He went on to say some kind and thoughtful words that will not mean much to anyone else, but they sure meant a lot to me. His sincere expressions of gratitude, acceptance, admiration, and love warmed my bones—all 206 of them! I immediately set my alarm to go off the next day so I could do the same for someone else. It would be difficult to avoid a relationship of collegiality with someone who gave you that kind of message.

One of these days at 2:06 I will call Sam, Corbin, and Cayden and tell them how proud I am of them for uniting so many in service and love. I will say, "I think it is remarkable that kids your age are doing so much good and encouraging so many others from all different walks of life and backgrounds to join you as colleagues. Keep it up, my friends!"

CIVILITY

Richard Beeman pointed out that those who attended the Constitutional Convention worked in a small and intimate space that by today's standards would have spelled certain disaster—definitely too close for comfort. Yet these men were able to be effective because they shared a commitment to civility (see *Plain, Honest Men*).

Civility is not only from the same root as the word *civilization,* but it is also one of the purposes of education. Thomas Groome wrote, "Ultimately education is a way of being with people" (*Christian Religious Education,* 137).

Ironically, at the time and place education formally begins, incivility quickly intrudes—elementary school classrooms and playgrounds. The following simple incident is typical. Two second-grade girls were playing on a swing set during recess. A third girl, wanting a swing, said to one of the swingers, "You shouldn't be playing with Lucy. She's not in the top math and reading groups, and *we* are." Fortunately, the child being addressed replied, "I like playing with Lucy. She is my friend." The uncivil child did not get the swing, but unfortunately, not all such schoolyard incidents end that well.

As education continues, some learn civility; others do not. One of my university colleagues was recently involved with a study of middle-school students who were having social and emotional difficulties. The particular students being studied were from ethnic and cultural minority backgrounds. After extensive interviews with the students, the researchers learned that one of the most frequent causes for problems was rude and demeaning behavior by other students. A common pattern was that a student of another ethnicity would taunt with a racial slur when there was no teacher close by to hear. If the victim responded with rude language or occasionally a physical shove or threat, the victim would be reported for starting a fight, and penalties including school suspension would be imposed. The academic as well as social and emotional development of a large number of students was being derailed by cruel, targeted incivility (Ellie Young, "School Experiences of Early Adolescent At-Risk Latino/a Youth").

Incivility often extends to adulthood. We see bad attitudes and behavior in the public discourse of politics, ethnicity, and religion. People divide up into their separate groups instead of seeing all of us as a part of the brotherhood of man. As we take this broader view, we see that we have more commonalities that unite us than differences that divide us. Practicing civility can not only help us recognize our commonalities, it can allow us to maximize each other's contributions.

I know of a young man who has taken a stand to promote civility. When McKay made the transition from elementary to middle school, he noticed that many of his peers had started using vulgar and offensive language—words they had not used when they were all together in elementary school. It bothered him enough that he decided to tell his friends to stop cussing. At age fourteen McKay started a "no cussing club" at his high school. At first his dad didn't like the idea because he was afraid it would make his son a target for bullying, but McKay was determined to confront the negative peer pressure, and his parents supported him. As his dad had predicted, McKay took some heat during

> *Practicing civility can not only help us recognize our commonalities, it can allow us to maximize each other's contributions.*

club signups, but when it was all over, more than a hundred teens had signed up to take his pledge. With the help of his uncle, McKay created a website called nocussing.com, and people all across the country started joining up.

The response bolstered his confidence, and McKay attended a city meeting where he was given time to explain to those present the extent of the problem. In response, the mayor of Los Angeles declared March 2–7, 2009, as "Cuss Free Week." That declaration became news, and McKay was invited to be a guest on *Good Morning America, The Tonight Show, Inside Edition,* and a long list of other TV shows. He received thousands of supportive emails—all because he decided not to swear and encouraged others in his school to do the same.

I wish that were the happy end of the story. Unfortunately, it's not. While many applauded McKay's efforts to promote civility, others did not. McKay became the focus of bullying at school and online as well. He has been called "the most cyberbullied kid in the world." His website has been hacked many times and infiltrated with insults, profanity, and pornography. He and his family have received death threats and bomb threats that were serious enough that police cars have been posted outside their home to provide protection. Seriously? A kid starts a no cussing club and receives death threats for it? Even McKay's father didn't foresee such intense reactions—especially from adults. Still McKay carries on. To date, his club boasts more than 20,000 members from all fifty states and thirty countries (see *The No Cussing Club*).

I can't help feeling that McKay would have fit in well at the Constitutional Convention. If George Washington were to send an email to McKay, I think he would approve of McKay's choices. Washington might even include the following statement, which he copied into a personal notebook from a translated version of a French book of etiquette and civility: "Every action in company ought to be with some sign of respect to those present. . . . Use no reproachful language against anyone, neither curses nor reviling" (in William J. Bennett, *The Spirit of America*, 152–53).

HUMILITY

Along with collegiality and civility, we owe the Constitution to the humility of men who were more concerned about advancing their country than themselves. Richard Beeman pointed out that while there were some representatives who left the convention in prideful huffs and others who refused to sign the final document, the majority of the representatives showed great humility. They were willing to bend and compromise when they could, and when they absolutely couldn't, they were still willing to listen, respect the viewpoints of others, and agree to disagree (see *Plain, Honest Men*).

Beyond Washington, Franklin, Madison, and Hamilton, some Americans would be hard pressed to remember the names of others who signed the document. Many of the humble signers would probably say that is as it should be. History has shown that the document as a whole has been more important than any individual's contribution. These men cared more about uniting the fiercely independent states than they worried about who would get the credit. Chris and Ted Stewart called the humility of these men *miraculous*: "specifically, the degree to which the delegates were willing to listen, to learn from one another, to compromise, and, when defeated, to accept the wisdom of their fellow delegates" (*Seven Miracles That Saved America*, 143). Similarly, Catherine Drinker Bowen wrote:

"In the Constitutional Convention the spirit of compromise reigned in grace and glory. . . . Men rise to speak and one sees them struggle with the bias of birthright, locality, statehood—South against North, East against West, merchant against planter. One sees them change their minds, fight against pride, and when the moment comes, admit their error" (*Miracle at Philadelphia*, xiv).

The humble representatives at the Constitutional Convention did not deny their talents, which were outstanding, or their experiences, which were varied and valuable. They offered these contributions to add to and enrich the contributions of the others for the benefit of all. Nineteenth-century English author John Ruskin wrote that "the first test of a truly great man is his humility." Ruskin explained, "I do not mean, by humility, doubt of his own power. . . . [Truly] great men . . . have a curious . . . feeling that . . .

greatness is not in them, but through them. . . . And they see something Divine . . . in every man they meet, and are endlessly, foolishly, incredibly merciful" (*The Works of John Ruskin*, 5:331).

As I watch modern political rivals clash, schools and businesses compete, and even Christian churches attack each other with venom, I believe it is time for all of us to seek more humility. The Apostle Paul compared believers to parts of a body. He wrote:

"But now are they many members, yet but one body. And the eye cannot say unto the hand, I have no need of thee: nor again the head to the feet, I have no need of you. Nay, much more those members of the body, which seem to be more feeble, are necessary. . . . And whether one member suffer, all the members suffer with it; or one member be honoured, all the members rejoice with it. Now ye are the body of Christ" (1 Corinthians 12:20–27).

Considering Paul's counsel, wouldn't it be wonderful to live in a world in which the pronoun *we* could replace *I* a little more often?

It was impressive to me to hear about a high school basketball player from Texas who showed great humility during a game. The coach at another high school had taken a boy, Mitchell, under his wing. Mitchell loved basketball, but

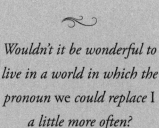

Wouldn't it be wonderful to live in a world in which the pronoun we *could replace* I *a little more often?*

due to a developmental disability, he didn't play on the team. Instead he acted as the team manager. In the last game of the regular season, the coach surprised Mitchell by telling him to suit up. The young man was proud to wear his school's jersey and cheer from the bench, but at the very end the coach sent Mitchell into the game. It was the moment he had dreamed of.

Mitchell's teammates did everything they could to get him the ball, but in his excitement he ended up throwing it out of bounds. That's when Jonathan, who was playing on the other team, was handed the ball to make an inbound pass. Jonathan's team was behind and needed to catch up, but instead of throwing the ball to one of his waiting teammates, Jonathan yelled Mitchell's name and passed the ball to him. Mitchell then turned and made a basket. The crowd went wild. Mitchell finally had his moment—a moment he will remember forever—facilitated by a caring coach and a young man from the opposing team who was humble enough to understand that by showing that kind of sportsmanship, everyone walked away a winner (see http://www. youtube.com/watch?v=sTaB-hPg0P4). When Jonathan was asked why he threw the ball to Mitchell, he said, "I was raised to treat others the way you want to be treated."

Some people say that Christianity has had its day and that the world has no more need for this out-of-step religion. They claim that Christianity has no place in a pluralistic society running at the speed of Twitter. Anyone who witnessed Jonathan's spontaneous and selfless act and heard his explanation might beg to differ. As would those who admire McKay's no cussing club. Anyone who feels that Christianity's message is irrelevant in today's world needs to meet Sam, Corbin, and Cayden Barlow and the hundreds of people these boys are uniting through acts of service and expressions of love.

Against today's pressure to accept worldly values, Christians can easily falter—especially when they stand alone. By standing together, we can be strong and show the world that the life, teachings, and example of Jesus Christ are not only timely, but timeless. C. S. Lewis wrote, "I believe in Christianity as I believe that the sun has risen, not only because I see it, but because by it I see everything else" (*The Weight of Glory,* 142). By developing the qualities of collegiality, civility, and humility, we demonstrate 7 days a week that Christianity is not a setting sun, but a rising sun bringing hope and light to the entire world.

CHAPTER TEN

❧

THE CORE OF CHRISTIANITY

I once overheard two college students having a discussion. The young woman was a devout Christian. The young man had grown up in a Christian home but announced that he had decided to follow an Eastern philosophy. The girl was shocked. "But you're such a nice person!" she exclaimed.

"Can't I do nice things without being Christian?" the young man asked. "Can't I have ethics and care about people without being Christian?" He went on to point out how after a tsunami in Japan—a primarily non-Christian country—there was no looting, while after an earthquake in Chile and a hurricane in the United States—primarily Christian countries—the looting was out of control. He spoke of knowing a Muslim who was a loving and devoted husband and father; in contrast, his own father, a "Christian," cheated on his mother, divorced her, paid no child support, "and yet he goes to church every Sunday."

My heart hurt for the disillusioned young man. There are too many like his father, as described by John Piper: "[They go] to church on Sunday and [have] a veneer of religion, but [their] religion is basically an add-on to the same way of life the world lives, not a transforming power. . . . They are cultural Christians. Religion is a formal, external thing. There has been no true inner awakening" (*Finally Alive*, 13, 17).

In addition to hurting for the young man, I also hurt for the young woman, who apparently assumed Christianity has a corner on the "nice" market. The Christian church is not a reservoir containing all the people who do good in the world. Actually, the gospel net gathers all kinds. As important as good deeds and extra miles may be, they are not the core of Christianity.

"The world can do almost anything as well as or better than the church," said George MacDonald. "You need not be a Christian to build houses, feed the hungry, or heal the sick. There is only one thing the world cannot do. It cannot offer grace" (as quoted by Philip Yancey, *What's So Amazing about Grace?* 15). The core of Christianity is the Atonement of Jesus Christ, who suffered and died on the cross so that we might live. The more we understand that core, the easier it is to avoid hurtful

> *As important as good deeds and extra miles may be, they are not the core of Christianity.*

hypocrisy and the veneer of cultural religion. The more personally we experience in our hearts the effects of Christ's sacrifice, the less content we are to see spirituality merely as ethics or as a kindness contest among religions.

As we learn of and accept Christ's ultimate gift, we can feel the inner awakening that makes all the difference. "I am come that they might have life," said the Savior, "and that they might have it more abundantly" (John 10:10). For the 7-day Christian, that joyful abundance is available every day of the week; it is not limited to Sundays. Christ's sacrifice offers us life after death, life after sin and disbelief, life amid trials, and, ultimately, life transformed.

LIFE AFTER DEATH

Was Jesus really raised from the dead? Did He actually resurrect? Did He show himself to His Apostles and others, as scriptures report? Some academics and historians express strong opinions one way or the other, but many claim it doesn't even matter. One man said to me, "Whether or not Jesus actually resurrected is a moot point. Yes or no, it only has relevance in the next life." I disagreed. Knowledge of Christ's resurrection not only changes the hereafter, it can also change what we are here after. It can profoundly affect our choices, our loves, our priorities, and our ways of reaching our potential.

When my father-in-law, Leroy Gunnell, passed away following surgery, one of the nurses in the intensive care unit noticed a big difference between how our family handled that moment and how another family just down the hall handled a similar situation. The nurse said, "In one room there was peace and perspective, and in the other room there was despair and hopelessness." Of course, our family felt great sadness at the passing of our father, but we also felt confident in the continuation of life and the promised resurrection. Because Jesus rose from the tomb, our father will also be resurrected. Lacking this understanding, the family down the hall was engulfed by overwhelming grief. For them, this passing was final.

As I spoke at Dad's funeral, I said, "I am grateful this nurse could see the difference, because it is that difference that Dad taught about throughout his life." Everyone who knew him understood that the source of the peace and perspective he enjoyed in his life and the peace and perspective that gave us comfort at his passing was the life, death, and resurrection of Jesus Christ.

"If a man die, shall he live again?" (Job 14:14). The question recorded in the Old Testament has been asked throughout the centuries. The answer is clear: "For as in Adam all die, even so in Christ shall all be made alive" (1 Corinthians 15:22). Christ's resurrection gives all of us the opportunity to continue living after we die. In recognition of this truth, my mother, Val C. Wilcox, wrote the following poem, which she titled "After Life":

It used to be
that theaters would show
a short-reel cartoon
where Bugs Bunny
would always outwit
Elmer Fudd and win,
before the final words
THE END.
It was only then
that the wide-screen,
technicolor
main feature could begin.

LIFE AFTER SIN AND DISBELIEF

Saul's conversion was dramatic. He "made havock of the church" by tormenting and persecuting its members. He punished those whose professed Christianity and "committed them to prison" (Acts 8:3). On his way to Damascus, "suddenly there shined round about him a light from heaven: And he fell to the earth, and heard a voice saying unto him, Saul, Saul, why persecutest thou me?" (Acts 9:3–4). Saul repented, left his past behind, was baptized, and began his ministry. The world would know him as Paul (see Acts 13).

Most conversions are less spectacular. Clive—known to his friends as Jack—was a bright boy born into a church-going family. As a young teen he began to view religion as a chore, and at the age of fifteen he announced he was an atheist. Jack later attended college, where he became friends with a firm believer whose arguments in favor of God and Christianity slowly began to influence him.

One day—not on his way to Damascus, but simply on a bus ride to the zoo—Jack experienced a quiet conversion. When he left for the zoo, he was an atheist. When he arrived, he was a Christian. The world would know Jack as C. S. Lewis, a powerful and prolific advocate of Christianity. Here is how Clive Staples Lewis, whose believing friend happened to be J. R. R. Tolkien, described his change of heart:

"I know very well when, but hardly how, the final step was taken. I was driven into Whipsnade one sunny morning. When we set out I did not believe that Jesus Christ is the Son of God, and when we reached the zoo I did. And yet I had not exactly spent the journey in thought. Nor in great emotion. 'Emotional' is perhaps the last word we can apply to some of the most important events. It was more like when a man, after long sleep, still lying motionless in bed, becomes aware that he is now awake" (*Surprised by Joy,* 237).

Dramatic or simple, in ancient times or modern, two men could say, "We know that we have passed from death unto life" (1 John 3:14). Their entire lives were altered, and both men stayed true to the end. Saul had committed grievous sins. Lewis had not deliberately wronged or persecuted anyone, but admitted he had been an angry, disbelieving teen and a proud, skeptical college student. Either way, the rebirth was necessary, the repentance sincere, and the forgiveness of heaven real. Both men recognized the error of their ways, turned to the Lord, and felt the promised joy of forgiveness—the newness of life that He alone can give (see 2 Corinthians 5:17). "Come now, and let us reason together, saith the Lord: though your sins be as scarlet, they shall be as white as snow; though they be red like crimson, they shall be as wool" (Isaiah 1:18).

LIFE AMID TRIALS

Along with the hope of resurrection and the joy of forgiveness, Christ's selfless sacrifice is also the source of comfort and consolation during trials. Christ is willing to succor us—to come to our aid—during our suffering. Sometimes suffering is the consequence of our own poor choices or the poor choices of others. Sometimes suffering is not necessarily due to anyone's choice, but results from mistakes or accidents; or it just occurs because this earthly journey includes devastating storms and deadly diseases. Whatever the challenges, Christ offers His divine help. Tenderly He teaches the lessons to be found within life's tests, however difficult and heart wrenching they may be.

In the summer of 1987, while my mother was undergoing an evaluation for diabetes, she had a screening mammogram that revealed a suspicious area in her left breast. A subsequent biopsy confirmed the diagnosis of cancer. She was sixty-two years old at the time. A partial mastectomy was scheduled. Mom tried to maintain a positive attitude, but in her journal she wrote, "I hate this raw intrusion in my life! If I could I would run from this on lightning shoes. I cannot overcome the sobbing fear that no more years remain for me."

The night before her surgery, family members gathered to ask for God's blessings and comfort. Mom wrote, "In answer to all prayers, a calm descended and I finally felt the peace of soul that cannot be described. I now am willing to place myself into the care of those whose hands will do the cutting that can save."

As Mom recovered from the surgery, she was a little shocked and discouraged about her disfigured body, but she savored her new perspective on life. She wrote in her journal, "And now I vow that ordinary days, delivered every morning just on time, will be received with purest gratitude and constant joy!"

Mom was true to her vow. It helped her endure difficult months of radiation therapy. It also helped her deal with the doctors' warnings that, regardless of all she had been through, the cancer could return. Again in the privacy of her journal Mom wrote, "Despite dismal prognosis that narrows my future to an imminent demise, I will go to work as always to do and try, to get and give." She found her comfort in knowing that the Savior had suffered for her—not just for her sins, but also for her pains and infirmities. She loved the Savior's words:

"Peace I leave with you, my peace I give unto you: not as the world giveth, give I unto you. Let not your heart be troubled, neither let it be afraid" (John 14:27).

"Observe all things whatsoever I have commanded you: and, lo, I am with you alway[s], even unto the end of the world" (Matthew 28:20).

Mom didn't just read those words. She took them personally. She felt the strength of the words and the strength of the speaker of those words. She said, "I am *not* going to spend whatever time I have left living to die, but rather dying to live!" The cancer never did return, and Mom made a full recovery.

Because of her cancer, Mom never dreamed she would outlive my father. When Dad passed away, Mom once again depended heavily on the consolation available through Christ's sacrifice. About a year after Dad's death, a well-meaning friend asked my mom, "When did you feel like Christ stepped in and made your burden bearable?"

She responded, "When didn't He? Was there ever a time when He wasn't shouldering the whole load?"

Just before her own passing at age eighty-eight, Mom struggled yet again, this time with dementia. When friends asked me how she was doing, I usually responded, "Her body is weak, but her spirit is strong." I'm told that as people age, they lose their filter for what is socially acceptable. They cannot hide their real opinions, beliefs, and feelings, appropriate or not. If that is the case, Mom was in pretty good shape. She may not have remembered to whom she was speaking, but she was always kind and full of love. She may not have been able to tell you what day it was, but she prayed every day with a faith that was unshakable.

LIFE TRANSFORMED

All Christ's gifts of life—life after death, life after sin, and life amid trials—are given deeper meaning in His promise of life "more abundantly" (John 10:10). Through the Atonement of Jesus Christ we can be resurrected, forgiven, and consoled, but we can also be transformed.

I once met a Chinese woman who, along with her husband and son, had immigrated to Melbourne, Australia. They had sold all they had in China and were living very humbly in their new home. They struggled to learn English and to find new friends. Also they had begun to show interest in Christianity. When I met this strong and intelligent young mother, I was impressed. Through a translator, I asked her why she was willing to sacrifice so much. Without a pause, she answered, "Because I want to give my son the opportunity for a better life." I couldn't help but imagine that Christ's answer to the same question would be similar: "I sacrificed because I want to give *you* the opportunity for a better life."

We cannot resurrect ourselves. We cannot wipe away our own sins and skepticism. We cannot reach into our own broken hearts and heal them. All these are gifts of grace. We cannot transform ourselves. Christ's grace—His divine help, His enabling power—is absolutely necessary. Those who say "I can do it myself" have not yet learned how truly powerless they are. Those who say "God helps those who help themselves" have yet to learn that God helps us *to* help ourselves. Those who only "say grace" at the dinner table have yet to learn that grace is not something we offer God; it is something we receive from Him. Those who feel they have fallen from grace have yet to learn that grace is actually what catches them and lifts them up.

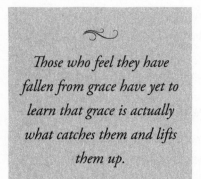

Those who feel they have fallen from grace have yet to learn that grace is actually what catches them and lifts them up.

I once received the following email from a friend named Jon: "As a young man I had a very difficult time coming to terms with my inevitable and continual state of imperfection, regardless of my good intentions and no matter how hard I worked at doing everything I was asked to do and being everything I was expected to be. . . . I often felt completely inadequate and insufficient."

People would tell Jon, "Just try your hardest. Do your best, and then let God do all the rest." It is a clever little rhyme, but for someone with Jon's perfectionist tendencies, even trying his hardest and doing his best seemed like overwhelming expectations. His email continued:

"Such well-intentioned advice was almost crippling to me. I knew I could always try just a little harder and do a little more. I felt that Christ's suffering and grace, even the companionship of the Holy Spirit, could only apply to me after I first rid myself of all ungodliness."

We can find ourselves feeling like Jon—unworthy of God's help—because we all fail in one way or another to meet His standards. We are weak and sinful, and we waver in our commitments. As we see how far we have to go, we feel like giving up. Thankfully, when we see only responsibilities, grace allows us to also see possibilities. Perhaps we have wrongly seen grace as the light at the end of the tunnel instead of the light that can surround us now and move us through the tunnel. Mike McKinley explained, "You will never be righteous enough to please God. But thankfully, Christ's perfect righteousness becomes ours when we come to him in faith" (*Am I Really a Christian?* 27).

We receive God's gift of grace by turning to Him in faith. We may doubt our own abilities, but we can't doubt His. It is through His grace that we can repent of our wrongdoings and strive to keep His commandments. Christ said, "If ye love me, keep my commandments" (John 14:15). It is through His grace that we recognize the presence of the Holy Spirit in our lives and are able to endure to the end. John Piper has written, "[We] are being changed, even if slowly, from one degree of humility and love to the next" (*Finally Alive,* 21). Similarly, Mike McKinley asked, "How can we know who the real believers are? How can we distinguish them from those with superficial professions of faith? Real believers endure until the end. Their attachment to Christ perseveres and never goes away" (*Am I Really a Christian?* 79).

How do we maintain faith, repent, and keep commandments, recognize the Spirit, and endure—especially in a world where many who label themselves as Christians have given up trying? The power comes from Christ Himself. We do not act in an effort to be worthy of grace. We act because we are enabled by grace. The same Christ who gives commands to obey is also the One who empowers us to obey. "Just as believers' salvation is not their own doing, neither is their perseverance. The amazing grace which saves wretches is the same amazing grace that brings them home" (Mike McKinley, *Am I Really a Christian?* 87).

Choosing to live as a daily disciple—a 7-day Christian—leads to significant personal development as we experience the Savior's transforming power. The grace that saves us is also the grace that changes us.

My daughter Whitney once pointed out to me that the parable of the talents—which I had always thought of as applying only to abilities or money—may also apply to the gift of Christ's grace.

"For the kingdom of heaven is as a man travelling into a far country, who called his own servants, and delivered unto them his goods. And unto one he gave five talents, to another two, and to another one" (Matthew 25:14–15).

The servants who received five and two used the gifts they were given and showed growth. The servant who received one was afraid and didn't use the gift. When the

Lord returned, he was pleased with the first two servants for expanding or enhancing what they had been given. He was not too concerned about how much their talents had grown or whose had grown the most, only that what he had given had been utilized (see vv. 16–23). When the servant who received one talent reported that his talent remained unchanged, the Lord called him "wicked and slothful" (v. 26). The servant had been given a gift but had neglected it (see 1 Timothy 4:14).

Now let us consider that perhaps the Lord was more concerned with improving servants than with multiplying talents. Let's say the talents represent the Lord's gift of grace. From this view, maybe *wicked* and *slothful* were not harsh words spoken in anger but realistic descriptions of attributes the third servant should have and could have changed. He had been given all he needed, but he had done nothing with it. Had he depended on God's grace, surely he could have become "good and faithful" like the others (v. 23).

In the parable, the Lord told the first two servants, "I will make thee ruler[s] over many things" (vv. 21, 23). Because the words were spoken after the reckoning, we assume their crowning as rulers happened after the servants had entered into the joy of their Lord. However, looking at it another way, perhaps the Lord had been making the faithful servants rulers all along. Maybe the reason the slothful servant was not allowed to enter was not because he was being punished but because he was unprepared. The term *ruler* may not have been a prize or title the servants were given as much as a description of who, through God's grace, they had become.

In the parable we read, "For unto every one that hath shall be given, and he shall have abundance" (v. 29). As the Lord said on a different occasion, "I am come that they might have life, and that they might have it more abundantly" (John 10:10).

THE END AND THE MEANS

"Come unto me," invited the Savior when He was on the earth (Matthew 11:28). Many apathetically ignored Him and went about living their lives. However, others flocked to Him. Was that enough? Was coming to Him the end? Some of those who initially accepted the invitation turned away, but others stayed and became His disciples. These faithful few knew that the true end of all Christians is not simply to come to Christ but to become Christlike.

In our day, many professed Christians still turn away. When one high-school coach was told about the serious misconduct of some of his players on an out-of-town trip, he said, "Looks like it's time for a little come-to-Jesus lecture." Perhaps what is needed most is not one more lecture about the importance of coming to Jesus, but

> *The true end of all Christians is not simply to come to Christ but to become Christlike.*

rather the assurance that He has come to us. His arms are extended to all—even misbehaving ballplayers. Christ is the means for resurrection, forgiveness and increased faith, peace amid pain, and transformation through it all.

Christ doesn't just want people in the church. He wants the church in people. He doesn't just want people to acknowledge His grace. He wants them to be transformed through it. He doesn't just want people to come to Him. He wants them to become like Him—a process that takes place 7 days a week, 52 weeks a year, and throughout all the years of our lives.

Sources

Beeman, Richard. *Plain, Honest Men: The Making of the American Constitution.* New York: Random House, 2009.

Bennett, William J. *The Spirit of America.* New York: Touchstone, 1997.

Bowen, Catherine Drinker. *Miracle at Philadelphia.* Boston: Little, Brown and Company, 1966.

Clark, Dan. "The Team and the Trophy." *Reader's Digest,* May 2013.

Covey, Stephen R. *The 7 Habits of Highly Effective People.* New York: Simon and Schuster, 1989.

Dew, Sheri. *No Doubt about It.* Salt Lake City: Bookcraft, 2001.

Fellowship of the Ring (DVD), directed by Peter Jackson. Los Angeles: Warner Brothers, 2001.

Francis, James Allan. *The Real Jesus and Other Sermons.* Philadelphia: Judson Press, 1926.

Givens, Terryl, and Fiona Givens. *The God Who Weeps.* Salt Lake City: Ensign Peak, 2012.

Groome, Thomas. *Christian Religious Education: Sharing Our Story and Vision.* San Francisco: Jossey-Bass, 1999.

Hafen, Bruce C. *A Disciple's Life: The Biography of Neal A. Maxwell.* Salt Lake City: Deseret Book, 2002.

Hatch, McKay. *The No Cussing Club.* South Pasadena, CA: Dawson Publishing, 2009.

Hawkes, Sharlene Wells. *Living in but Not of the World.* Salt Lake City: Deseret Book, 1997.

Hugo, Victor. *Les Misérables.* Reprint edition. Norwich, UK: Canterbury Classics, 2013.

Kinnaman, David, and Gabe Lyons. *UnChristian: What a New Generation Really Thinks About Christianity . . . and Why It Matters.* Grand Rapids, MI: Baker Books, 2007.

Lewis, C. S. *The Chronicles of Narnia, Book 2: Prince Caspian.* New York: Collier Books, 1970.

———. *Surprised by Joy: The Shape of My Early Life.* New York: Harcourt Brace, 1955.

———. *The Weight of Glory and Other Addresses.* New York: Macmillan, 1980.

Liberty Institute. "Student Suspended." Accessed online at http://www.libertyinstitute.org/pages/florida-atlantic-university-student-suspended.

Lloyd, R. Scott. "Elder Holland Says to Live Gospel in Small Ways." *Deseret News,* September 10, 2012.

MacArthur, John F., Jr. *Faith Works: The Gospel According to the Apostles.* Dallas: Word Publishing, 1993.

Maxwell, Neal A. *A Time to Choose.* Salt Lake City: Deseret Book, 1972.

McKinley, Mike. *Am I Really a Christian?* Wheaton, IL: Crossway, 2011.

Momen, Tito, and Jeff Benedict. *My Name Used to Be Muhammad: The True Story of a Muslim Who Became a Christian.* Salt Lake City: Ensign Peak, 2013.

Murray, John A. "Where's God in Celebration of MLK?" *USA Today,* Thursday, August 15, 2013.

Neuhaus, Richard John. "C. S. Lewis in the Public Square." *First Things,* 88 (December 1998):30.

Newman, John H. *Newman Reader: Works of John Henry Newman.* The National Institute for Newman Studies, 2007. Accessed online at http://www.newmanreader.org/.

News Catcher 31. "College Student Suspended for Refusing to STOMP on Jesus Sign." Accessed online at http://www.youtube.com/watch?v=nmPDGL1XYlA.

Peale, Norman Vincent. *The Power of Positive Thinking.* New York: Prentice Hall, 1954.

Pearce, Virginia H. "Creating a Relationship with God." In *A Year of Powerful Prayer: Getting Answers for Your Life Every Day.* Salt Lake City: Deseret Book, 2013.

Pinegar, J. Michael. "The Lord's Goods." Speech delivered November 16, 2004, at Brigham Young University. Accessed online at speeches.byu.edu.

Piper, John. *Finally Alive.* Scotland, Great Britain: Christian Focus, 2009.

Rath, Tom, and Donald O. Clifton. *How Full Is Your Bucket?* Omaha, NE: Gallup Press, 2004.

Roosevelt, Eleanor. *You Learn by Living: Eight Keys for a More Fulfilling Life.* Fiftieth anniversary edition. New York: Harper Perennial, 2011.

Rowling, J. K. *Harry Potter and the Sorcerer's Stone.* New York: Scholastic, 1997.

Ruskin, John. *The Works of John Ruskin*. 39 vols. Edited by E. T. Cook and Alexander Wedderburn. London, UK: George Allen, 1903–12.

Stewart, Chris, and Ted Stewart. *The Miracle of Freedom: 7 Tipping Points That Saved the World*. Salt Lake City: Shadow Mountain, 2011.

———. *Seven Miracles That Saved America: Why They Matter and Why We Should Have Hope*. Salt Lake City: Shadow Mountain, 2009.

Tolkien, J. R. R. *The Lord of the Rings*. Fiftieth anniversary edition. New York: Houghton Mifflin Harcourt, 2004.

Ulrich, Wendy. "Not Ashamed." In *The Temple Experience: Passage to Healing and Holiness*. Springville, UT: Cedar Fort, Inc., 2012, 99–118.

———. "The Presence of an Absence." In *The Temple Experience: Passage to Healing and Holiness*. Springville, UT: Cedar Fort, Inc., 2012, 167–82.

USnews.nbcnews.com. "Florida School Apologizes." Accessed online at http://usnews.nbcnews.com/_news/2013/03/27 /17485007-florida-school-apologizes-after-students-stomp -on-jesus?lite.

Yancey, George. *Compromising Scholarship: Religious and Political Bias in American Higher Education*. Waco, TX: Baylor University Press, 2011.

Yancey, Philip. *What's So Amazing about Grace?* Grand Rapids, MI: Zondervan, 1977.

Yee, Paul Yensing. "No Laughing Matter?" *Reader's Digest,* June 2013.

Young, Ellie. "School Experiences of Early Adolescent At-Risk Latino/a Youth." Manuscript in process, 2013.